WORD ONE

SADLER HAYLLAR POWELL

M

Copyright © R. K. Sadler, T. A. S. Hayllar, C. J. Powell 1979

Drawings by Don Porter

All rights reserved.
No part of this publication
may be reproduced or transmitted,
in any form or by any means,
without permission.

First published 1979 by
THE MACMILLAN COMPANY OF AUSTRALIA PTY LTD
107 Moray Street, South Melbourne 3205
6 Clarke Street, Crows Nest 2065
Reprinted 1980, 1981, 1982 (twice), 1983 (three times), 1984 (twice), 1985, 1986

Associated companies and representatives throughout the world.

National Library of Australia
cataloguing in publication data
Sadler, Rex Kevin.
 Word skills one.
 ISBN 0 333 29872 1
 1. English language – Composition and exercises.
 I. Hayllar, Thomas Albert S., joint author. II. Powell,
 Clifford J., joint author. III. Title.
428
Set in Plantin and Optima by The Markby Group
Printed in Hong Kong

Contents

Preface   v

1. The Wolves   1
   Little House on the Prairie (Laura Ingalls Wilder)

2. Landing   7
   To the Wild Sky (Ivan Southall)

3. Shaggy Dog   15
   A Dog Called George (Margaret Balderson)

4. A Hold-Up   23
   Midnite (Randolph Stow)

5. Some Pig!   31
   Charlotte's Web (E. B. White)

6. The Waterspout   41
   Blue Fin (Colin Thiele)

7. A Crazy Conversation   49
   Freaky Friday (Mary Rodgers)

8. The Devilfish   57
   Island of the Blue Dolphins (Scott O'Dell)

9. At the Playground   63
   The October Child (Eleanor Spence)

10. Flying Machine   71
    Flambards (K. M. Peyton)

11. The Nargun   81
    The Nargun and the Stars (Patricia Wrightson)

12. Torpedoed   89
    The Cay (Theodore Taylor)

13. Bush Fire   95
    Wildfire (Mavis Thorpe Clark)

14. Eating the Evidence   103
    The Goal-Keeper's Revenge and Other Stories (Bill Naughton)

15. The Death of Beowulf — 111
    Dragon Slayer (Rosemary Sutcliff)

16. The World's Worst Whinger — 117
    The Yarns of Billy Borker (Frank Hardy)

17. The Hiding Place — 125
    The Silver Sword (Ian Serraillier)

18. A Brumby Fight — 131
    The Brumby (M. E. Patchett)

19. Pursuit by a Grizzly Bear — 139
    Children on the Oregon Trail (A. Rutgers van der Loeff)

20. Frightful the Falcon — 147
    My Side of the Mountain (Jean George)

21. The Planes — 155
    The Dolphin Crossing (Jill Paton Walsh)

22. Night Terrors — 161
    Sam and Me (Joan Tate)

23. Saved — 169
    Dorp Dead (Julia Cunningham)

24. Disaster on the Lawn — 175
    Beasts in my Belfry (Gerald Durrell)

25. The Wild Ones — 185
    The Men from P.I.G. and R.O.B.O.T. (Harry Harrison)

26. A Viking Raid — 193
    Horned Helmet (Henry Treece)

27. Death of a Roo — 203
    Dingo (Henry G. Lamond)

Dictionary — 210

Acknowledgements — 218

Preface

An important aim of *Word Skills One* is to expose students to the writing of a wide range of exciting and respected practitioners of words. As well as serving as excellent models for students, these writers have the potential to capture student interest so that students will read the book from which the extract is taken. It is our hope that, because of the exciting, even compelling, nature of these passages, this will tend to happen. In line with this, if a class library can be established, incorporating as many of these titles as possible, this will perfectly fit our hopes. The writers represented here are outstanding as authors of books for young people.

Word Skills One, as the title suggests, is also aimed at developing students' skills in their use of language. It provides opportunities for junior secondary students to work with words in as many interesting and varied ways as possible, so that their competence and creativity in the use of language are enhanced. To this end, we have included, among other exercises, those which require the following skills: comprehension, vocabulary extension, selection of the correct form of words, experimentation with sentence structure, searching for expressive and appropriate words, identification and creation of similes and apt comparisons, identification of practical linguistic features of words, and using correct spelling and punctuation. Exercises in each unit derive from the opening passage. Each of these passages is an extract from a book geared to the level and interest of students.

Word Skills One unashamedly requires students to be busy in working with words. Among the many insights that have come from learning theory and the field of special education is the truth that there is no substitute for practice. Mastery in any skill area comes from practice.

Little House on the Prairie

Laura Ingalls Wilder

1. The Wolves

'Little House on the Prairie' tells of the journey westward of a family of white settlers to the wild and lonely Indian country, where they eventually build their log house. In this passage, Pa describes to the family his terrifying encounter with a pack of wolves.

Pa took a short cut across the prairie, and as he was loping along on Patty, suddenly out of a little draw came a pack of wolves. They were all around Pa in a moment.

'It was a big pack,' Pa said. 'All of fifty wolves, and the biggest wolves I ever saw in my life. Must be what they call buffalo wolves. Their leader's a big grey brute that stands three feet at the shoulder, if an inch. I tell you my hair stood straight on end.'

'And you didn't have your gun,' said Ma.

'I thought of that. But my gun would have been no use if I'd had it. You can't fight fifty wolves with one gun. And Patty couldn't outrun them.'

'What did you do?' Ma asked.

'Nothing,' said Pa. 'Patty tried to run. I never wanted anything worse than I wanted to get away from there. But I knew if Patty even started, those wolves would be on us in a minute, pulling us down. So I held Patty to a walk.'

'Goodness, Charles!' Ma said under her breath.

'Yes. I wouldn't go through such a thing again for any money. Caroline, I never saw such wolves. One big fellow trotted along, right by my stirrup. I could have kicked him in the ribs. They didn't pay any attention to me at all. They must have just made a kill and eaten all they could.

'I tell you, Caroline, those wolves just closed in around Patty and me and trotted along with us. In broad daylight. For all the world like a pack of dogs going along with a horse. They were all around us, trotting along, and jumping and playing and snapping at each other, just like dogs.'

'Goodness, Charles!' Ma said again. Laura's heart was thumping fast, and her mouth and her eyes were wide open, staring at Pa.

'Patty was shaking all over, and fighting the bit,' said Pa. 'Sweat ran off her, she was so scared. I was sweating, too. But I held her down to a walk, and we went walking along among those wolves.

They came right along with us, a quarter of a mile or more. That big fellow trotted by my stirrup as if he were there to stay.

'Then we came to the head of a draw, running down into the creek bottoms. The big grey leader went down it, and all the rest of the pack trotted down into it, behind him. As soon as the last one was in the draw, I let Patty go.

'She headed straight for home, across the prairie. And she couldn't have run faster if I'd been cutting into her with a rawhide whip. I was scared the whole way. I thought the wolves might be coming this way and they might be making better time than I was. I was glad you had the gun, Caroline. And glad the house is built. I knew you could keep the wolves out of the house with the gun.'

LAURA INGALLS WILDER, *Little House on the Prairie*

1. Reading for Meaning

(a) How did Pa first react to being surrounded by wolves?
(b) What was Pa's attitude to using a gun on the wolves?
(c) What reason does Pa give for the wolves not attacking him and Patty?
(d) In what ways did the wolves act like dogs?
(e) How did Laura react to Pa's story?
(f) What reasons did Pa have for hurrying home?
(g) What reasons did Pa have for thinking his family would be safe?
(h) Why does Pa say, 'I wouldn't go through such a thing again for any money'?
(i) Do you like this story? Why?
(j) What is the meaning of:
    (i) prairie   (ii) galloping   (iii) loping   (iv) rawhide?
You may need to use the back-of-the-book dictionary.

2. In the Right Order

The events below are jumbled up. Re-arrange them in their correct order.
(a) Pa lets Patty go as fast as her legs will carry them.
(b) The wolves pay no attention to Pa.
(c) The wolves go down into the creek bottoms.
(d) Suddenly out of a little draw comes a pack of wolves.
(e) Patty tries to run but Pa holds her to a walk.
(f) Laura and Ma are both amazed and fearful.
(g) Pa decides to take a short cut home across the prairie.

3. Words of your Own

Write down these sentences from the story and replace the words in heavy print with words of your own that have a similar meaning.
(a) They **were all around** Pa **in a moment**.
(b) All of fifty wolves, and the **biggest** I ever **saw** in my life.
(c) Patty couldn't **outrun** them.
(d) I wouldn't **go through** such a thing for any money.
(e) One big fellow trotted along, **right by** my stirrup.
(f) They **didn't pay any attention** to me.
(g) I was **glad** you had the gun.
(h) My gun would have been **no use** if I'd had it.
(i) Laura's heart was **thumping** fast.
(j) Patty **tried** to run.

4. Subjects

In the left-hand column is a list of subjects. Write each one down and add the correct ending from the right-hand list to make up a sentence from the story.

	SUBJECT	ENDING
(a)	My gun	trotted by my stirrup.
(b)	Ma	couldn't outrun the wolves.
(c)	Laura's heart	would have been of no use.
(d)	The big wolf	was thumping fast.
(e)	The wolves	stood on end.
(f)	Pa	were snapping at each other.
(g)	Patty	said, 'Goodness, Charles'.
(h)	My hair	took a short cut across the prairie.

5. Complete the Sentences

Use your knowledge of the story to complete these sentences.
(a) Pa, who ...., was loping along on Patty.
(b) The pack of wolves, which ...., surrounded Pa in a moment.
(c) The wolves' leader, which ...., stood three feet at the shoulder if an inch.
(d) Pa could have kicked one big fellow, which ....
(e) Laura, whose ...., was staring at Pa.
(f) Caroline, who ...., would have been able to protect the family against the wolves.

6. Put the Sentences Back Together

These sentences have been taken from the story, but the words in each one have been jumbled up. Your job is to put each of the sentences back together. A good approach is first to find the verbs and their subjects.

(a) gun can't fifty fight with you wolves one.
(b) right stirrup big my by along one trotted fellow.
(c) tell end stood my on hair straight you I.
(d) for straight across the she home prairie headed.
(e) way I whole scared the was.
(f) keep house out gun wolves the I knew of you the could the with.

7. Using the Right Forms

Write down these sentences and complete them by inserting the correct form of the words in brackets.

(a) Pa's shock was only .... [moment]
(b) The .... of the wolves' arrival shocked Pa. [suddenly]
(c) Laura listened .... to Pa. [attention]
(d) Pa's gun was quite .... against the wolves. [use]
(e) Pa's .... warned him that it would be futile to fight fifty wolves. [knew]
(f) Pa believed his meeting with the wolves was one of the .... experiences he had ever had. [worse]
(g) Pa said that Patty shook all over and .... the bit. [fight]
(h) It was the .... Patty had ever run. [fast]

To the Wild Sky

Ivan Southall

2. Landing

It was bound to run out of petrol some time. The children seemed to have been in the plane for days waiting to die. And Gerald, who had taken the controls when the pilot died, just flew on, as though he didn't know how to land.

He knew that flaps had to be used for landing, but how and in what way? It would be better not to try. He might end up wrecking everything. He should have practised when he was up above the clouds. He had decided to do it, made up his mind to it, then the thought had melted away, Oh, golly. All that time up there and he hadn't done it.

1,200 feet now on the altimeter, but it wasn't right. He was lower than that. The water looked so close. There were breakers to be seen, distinctly. A shaft of fear pierced him.

The altimeter was certainly wrong and he was 200 yards offshore.

Almost in panic he touched the rudder with his left foot, skidded the *Egret* over, pleaded for the land to rush out to meet him. And it did. The curving shore swept into his path, but the breakers, now on his right, didn't seem to be closer. He had lost 200 feet and they looked the same as before.

Ninety knots. Much, much too fast. How to get it back? How to stay on course? How to follow the beach? Its direction was so changeable.

Eighty knots, but now the controls felt funny. He had too much engine on, that was it. He was up and down and all over the place like a roller-coaster.

Engine off! It had to be done. And he did it numbly, in terror, and at once the engine note changed and he felt the seat drop from under him. Felt himself sinking into a world of *trees*.

In wildest alarm, he realized he had lost the beach. Sixty knots. Where was the beach? The controls were so sloppy and there was nothing but trees. Fifty knots. Nothing but trees. She was going, going to fall, going to drop clean out of the sky.

'Oh, God, please,' he screamed. 'God please, I don't know where I am, I can't see.'

But the speed was still fifty knots and still he floated. It felt like a leaf falling, like a leaf fluttering into an emptiness that might never come to an end.

'We'll be killed,' he screamed, and then the *Egret* struck and everything was black and shapeless and violent. There was a blow in his back like a swing from a club and a roaring sound in his head and suddenly he was in the air again, where he didn't know, how he didn't know, except that the nose was in the air again and the sky was swimming with watery stars and the bottom seemed to be falling out of a world that was breaking apart.

A thought crowded in somewhere that he had hit the beach after all, not the trees, hit the beach at the water-line, and that the *Egret* had bounced like a punctured rubber ball. He knew he had to switch off, but couldn't find the switch, not quickly enough. He fumbled wildly, but struck again in an eruption of spray.

The engine expired in a discharge of water and sound and sparks and the *Egret* twisted as though spinning on a roundabout, buckling into sand and water like some huge animal with failing legs.

Then there was quiet. Everything was quiet except for the sound of children crying.

IVAN SOUTHALL, *To the Wild Sky*

1. Reading for Meaning

(a) What did Gerald suddenly realize he should have practised up above the clouds?
(b) Why did Gerald fail to practise up above the clouds?
(c) What caused him to distrust the altimeter?
(d) Was the altimeter wrong as Gerald suspected? What evidence is there to answer this?
(e) 'Felt himself sinking into a world of *trees*.' Explain why 'trees' is printed in italics.
(f) What indication is there that Gerald was starting to crack up under the pressure as he tried to bring the *'Egret'* down?
(g) What was Gerald concerned to do immediately after they had crash-landed?
(h) What evidence is there in the extract to suggest that there is more than one person in the plane?
(i) What caused the controls of the *'Egret'* to go sloppy?
(j) Why was the quiet so noticeable at the end?

2. Sentence Break-Up

The following groups of words were originally sentences in the extract. See if you can put them back together again as sentences. It is not necessary to make them exactly the same as they appear in the extract.

(a) pleaded for the land to rush out
   he touched the rudder with his left foot
   to meet him
   almost in panic
   skidded the *Egret* over

(b) had melted away
   he had decided to do it
   then the thought
   made up his mind to it

(c) like a leaf fluttering
   like a leaf falling
   it felt
   that might never come to an end
   into an emptiness

(d) not quickly enough
   he knew he had to switch off
   but couldn't find the switch

(e) of children crying
   everything was quiet
   except for the sound

(f) and everything was black
   and then the *Egret* struck
   and shapeless and violent
   'We'll be killed,' he screamed

(g) in terror
   from under him
   and he did it numbly
   and he felt the seat drop
   and at once the engine note changed

(h) going to fall
   clean out of the sky
   going to drop
   she was going

3. In the Right Order

The following incidents are in a jumbled order. Put them into the order in which they occur in the extract.

(a) Flying speed drops to eighty knots
(b) Gerald screams
(c) Gerald touches the rudder with his left foot
(d) Children start crying
(e) The sky appears to be swimming with watery stars
(f) Gerald regrets failing to practise landing earlier
(g) The controls first start to feel funny
(h) Gerald is hit in the back of the head
(i) Gerald switches the engine off
(j) The *Egret* crash-lands
(k) Gerald tries to switch off the engine
(l) 1,200 feet shows on the altimeter
(m) The plane engine dies

4. -SE and -CE Words

In the extract, Gerald wishes that he had taken time to *practise* landing up above the clouds. 'Practise' is one of those frequently-misspelt words that change their spelling from '*-ise*' (verb) to '*-ice*' (noun).

Here is a list of such words. Note the spelling each time.

VERB	NOUN
practise	practice
advise	advice
license	licence
prophesy	prophecy

Decide whether the noun or the verb is required in the following sentences and fill in the blanks with correctly-spelt words from the list. The first letter of each word is given.

Landing 11

(a) Gerald had no pilot's l................ but he was the only one who knew anything about flying.
(b) It was impossible for any of the others to a................ him as they knew nothing about flying.
(c) The end of the world is one p................ that has not yet come true.
(d) The tiny bit of p................ he had done when his father was flying was a start.
(e) 'I p................ that things will get better or worse.'
(f) He tried to remember the a................ given by his father the times they had flown.
(g) Even if he had had the skill his youthfulness would have meant they could not l................ him to fly.
(h) While they were still high enough he began to p................ banking, using the rudder pedals gently.

5. Vocabulary

Match each word in the list below with its correct meaning from the meanings column. Use the back-of-the-book dictionary if you need help.

	WORD	MEANING
(a)	distinctly	penetrated
(b)	eruption	inclined to alter; irregular
(c)	altimeter	an unloading; a release
(d)	pleaded	plainly; clearly
(e)	changeable	broad hinged piece on wings used to make plane rise or fall
(f)	discharge	aeronautical instrument for measuring height above sea level
(g)	expired	on the seaward side of the shore
(h)	pierced	a bursting forth; a breaking out
(i)	off-shore	breathed out; died
(j)	flaps	made earnest appeal to

12 Word Skills One

6. It's and Its

It's is a contraction of *it is* or *it has*. **Its** shows ownership for the word 'it'. *Its* means *of it*.

The simplest way to decide which to use is to ask: 'Can I substitute *it is* or *it has* in this sentence?' If you can, use *it's!* If you can't, use *its!*

Choose the correct word for each of the following sentences.

(a) [Its/It's] direction was so changeable.
(b) The plane at times seemed to have a mind of [its/it's] own.
(c) '[It's/Its] time to cut the engine,' thought Gerald.
(d) The *Egret* struck and bounced, [its/it's] nose in the air, then flopped into the water.
(e) '[Its/It's] now or never,' he realized, and cut the engine.

7. Similes

A **simile** is a figure of speech which compares two things by saying one is 'like' or 'as' another. Write out the following sentences from the passage and underline the similes they contain.

(a) He was up and down and all over the place like a roller-coaster.
(b) It felt like a leaf falling, like a leaf fluttering into an emptiness that might never come to an end.
(c) There was a blow in his back like a swing from a club and a roaring sound in his head.
(d) A thought crowded in somewhere that he had hit the beach after all, not the trees, hit the beach at the water-line, and that the *Egret* had bounced like a punctured rubber ball.
(e) The engine expired in a discharge of water and sand and sparks and the *Egret* twisted as though spinning on a roundabout, buckling into sand and water like some huge animal with failing legs.

Now make up your own similes to complete the following sentences.

(f) He could see that the propeller was bent like ....
(g) A pain as though .... wrenched his chest.
(h) Gerald recoiled from the dead man as ....
(i) The plane engine screamed like ....

8. Change-A-Word

Each of the words below is taken from the passage. By following the clues and shuffling the letters, you can change each word into a new word. The first one is done for you.

(a) FELT becomes 'the opposite of right'. LEFT
(b) NOTE becomes 'a quality of sound'. ....
(c) SEAT becomes 'what you enjoy at a party'. ....
(d) DROP becomes 'to poke'. ....
(e) TREES becomes 'to adjust the dials back to their original position'. ....
(f) EGRET becomes 'to welcome'. ....
(g) BLOW becomes 'a kind of dish'. ....
(h) SPRAY becomes 'speaks with God'. ....
(i) STILL becomes 'sounds gently up and down'. ....

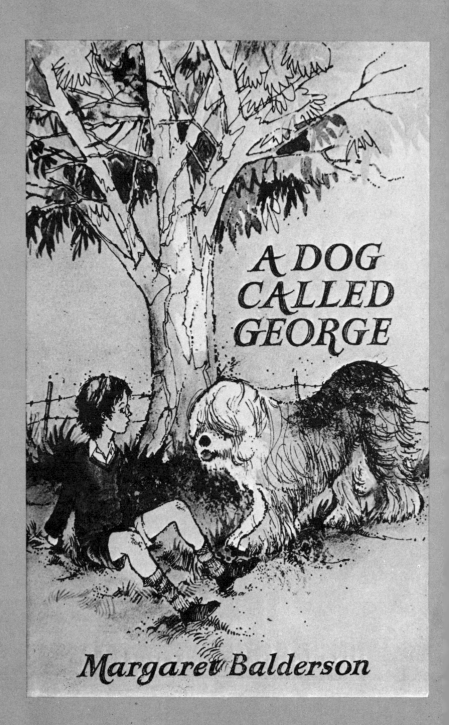

3. Shaggy Dog

Tony, acting out his imagination in the fog, stumbles into something that even his imagination can't quite handle . . .

The fog was very thick now. He couldn't see more than a few feet ahead of him. He watched in fascination as his own breath shot out in puffs of thin white vapour before his nose. He tried to suck it back in again. Then he huffed and puffed and blew till his glasses clouded over and he could feel a heavy moisture clinging to his brow.

Tony loved the fog. Within it he felt safe, protected and even anonymous in a nice, comfortable sort of way. You could pretend to be whoever you liked in the fog, and somebody standing only a few yards away would never know. You could be Tarzan swinging through the trees. You could be Neil Armstrong walking on the moon. You could be Douglas Bader in his Spitfire shooting down Messerschmitts over France.

Tony let out a triumphant screech and started zooming across the Runway. The Spitfire did some admirable stunts — wheeled, turned on its back, looped and dived as it circled the lower part of the Runway two or three times. Then, quite unexpectedly it braked and plummeted somewhat foolishly to its hands and knees with a surprised squawk.

'Wow!' stammered Tony in awe. For George, massive, magnificent and almost too much for one small, short-sighted boy to take in at a glance had suddenly loomed up in the mist before him.

He was sitting under Yogi Jim's tree. He was staring fixedly at the ground. He was the most extraordinary animal that Tony had ever seen.

'Wow!' said Tony again. The dog turned its great white blob of a head towards him for a moment and then stared back at the ground.

'Hey — what you looking at, fella?' asked Tony. He crawled across on his hands and knees to where the dog was sitting and looked, too. There was nothing but the usual sorts of things. Lots of brown frost-bitten grass, a screwed-up cigarette packet, a dollop of stale bubble-gum and a couple of soggy bus tickets.

Tony looked at the dog and the dog looked back at Tony. He began to feel uncomfortable. There was something rather disturbing about being stared at by a face that had no eyes.

'You gotta have eyes. Everything's got eyes,' said Tony.

He began pulling back layer upon layer of the dog's shaggy white hair until he found what he was looking for. At first he couldn't believe it. The eyes were blue — pale blue, like marbles, with short, bristly eyebrows and fleshy pink rims.

'Dogs all have brown eyes. What's the matter with you?' complained Tony indignantly.

The dog opened its mouth and an alarming quantity of slippery pink tongue rolled out. Then it retrieved the whole lot with one clean snap of its unseen jaws and resumed its inspection of the ground.

Tony took out his handkerchief and wiped his glasses.

'You lost or something, fella?' he asked amiably.

The dog lifted its paw and slapped it down hard into Tony's proffered hand.

Tony blinked.

'Pleased to meet you, I'm sure,' he said, placing the paw back firmly on the ground where it belonged.

The paw came up again. There was something almost clockwork about its movement. Tony was intrigued. He had a deep respect for all things mechanical.

'O.K., O.K., shake hands,' he crooned obligingly.

But the paw came up for the third time. It was getting monotonous.

'All right, so you're clever,' he admitted grudgingly. 'But, I once saw a dog in a circus jump through a burning hoop. Bet you couldn't do that.'

The dog hung his head. A very small pink triangle of tongue was showing now. It seemed to suggest that the blob was concentrating. Though whether it was or not, Tony couldn't say.

For a moment Tony doubted whether it was real. There was something about it that made him think very positively of soft toys — those big, bulky, comfortable soft toys that appeared so miraculously every Christmas in the shop windows down in Civic. Brushed nylon stuffed with bits of foam rubber — that's all it was, he suddenly decided. But then the dog broke into a rhythm of deep mechanical puffs, and he had to admit that although he'd seen talking dolls and squeaking teddy-bears, nobody had come up yet with a panting pooch. At least he'd never heard of one.

MARGARET BALDERSON, *A Dog Called George*

Shaggy Dog 17

1. Reading for Meaning

(a) What made it possible for Tony to be whoever he liked?
(b) Name the three men of action that Tony pretends to be.
(c) What causes Tony, as a Spitfire, to come to a sudden, squawking stop?
(d) Why does Tony find George's stare rather disturbing?
(e) What, at first, is unbelievable about George's face?
(f) Explain what happens when the dog opens its mouth.
(g) How does George make the first move towards friendship?
(h) 'Tony was intrigued.' By what?
(i) The 'blob' is a name for a part of George. What part and why is it appropriate?
(j) What sudden activity makes Tony admit to himself that George must be a real dog?

2. Dictionary Work

(a) Look up the following words in your back-of-the-book dictionary.

anonymous	amiably	proffered
monotonous	retrieved	intrigued
plummeted	indignantly	admirable

(b) Rewrite the following paragraphs using the correct words from the box as you do so.

In the fog, Tony felt .... and therefore able to pretend to be anyone or anything he chose. He was acting out a fighter plane doing some .... stunts when he stalled and .... to a crawl in front of George.
　Tony was .... by the dog. Even so, he did complain .... about his curious eyes. Tony also noticed that the dog had a habit of letting his tongue flop out but then he .... it with a snap of his jaws.
　Feeling friendly but curious as to why George stared at the ground, Tony .... asked him if he'd lost something. George, by way of reply, dropped his paw into Tony's .... hand. Each time Tony pushed it away, George replaced it with .... regularity.

18 Word Skills One

3. Describing George

By describing this and that about George, the writer builds us a living, breathing picture of the magnificent dog as seen by Tony. It's all done with the right word in the right place. Let's work on it.

Draw George in your workbook. Then, using the Long Line of Words, complete the descriptions.

GEORGE

First Impression:
....., ...

Hair: ....

Eyes:
Head:
Mouth:
Tongue:

Colour: ....
Compared to: .....
Eyebrows: ....., ...
Rims: ....
....
....
....
....

THE LONG LINE OF WORDS:

```
p s p b s   m g p p m m w p b d t s s   m b f w
u h i l l   a r a i e a h i l e r h m a r l h
f a n o i s e l n c g i n u e i o a r i e i
f g k b p s a e k h n t k e p a r l b s s t
s   g     p i t       a i e       n t l l t h e
    y       e v       n f         g     e l y
            r e       i i         l     s y
            y         c c         e
                      a e
                      l n
                        t
```

4. Shapes in the Fog

Here's a list of twenty spelling words from the passage (including dictionary words):

> fascination
> vapour
> moisture
> anonymous
> triumphant
> admirable
> plummeted
> fixedly
> extraordinary
> believe
> indignantly
> retrieved
> handkerchief
> amiably
> proffered
> intrigued
> monotonous
> grudgingly
> miraculously
> rhythm

Here are three 'shapes in the fog'. Copy them into your workbook, then fill in all **the 21** words. Strategic letters placed on the shapes are your clues.

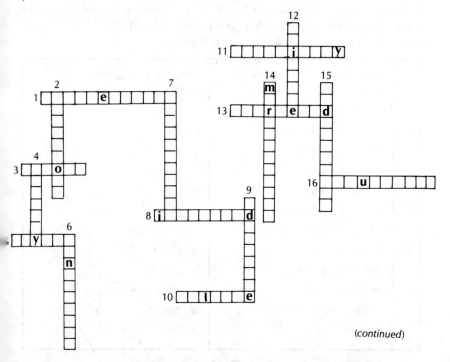

(continued)

20 Word Skills One

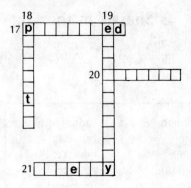

5. Just Right

Often, more than a single word is needed to explain exactly what you mean. Sometimes, however, one word will prove to be 'just right'. In the passage there are many such words, so here's an exercise that's just right for them.

For the several words on the left, supply the word that is just right. To help you, the first letter of the word and also the rest of the word's letters (jumbled) are given. For further help and to check up on your words, turn to the back-of-the-book dictionary.

	THE SEVERAL WORDS	THE JUST RIGHT WORD
(a)	went round and round	c eldric
(b)	in the near future	s ono
(c)	made an effort	t idre
(d)	not very many	f we
(e)	at the present time	n wo
(f)	without any warning	u pydtexcelen
(g)	dropped out of the sky	p medmutle
(h)	large and heavy	m viseas
(i)	not a single thing	n gitohn
(j)	thinking hard	c gtrocnitnean
(k)	hidden from sight	u nesne
(l)	own up	a timd

6. Action in the Fog

Verbs are absent from the following summary of *A Dog Called George*. You can see where they've been but now they are milling around in the fog. Rewrite the passage, putting back the verbs correctly.

.... by his brighter brothers and sister, Tony .... insecure and dissatisfied until the day he .... upon George .... beneath a tree and apparently as solitary as Tony himself. George .... an Old English sheepdog — blue-eyed, shaggy, ... with exuberant energy, an affectionate, mischievous companion. Through George, life .... on new colour and meaning for Tony, for the dog .... a focus of attention wherever he ...., ... him new friends and new interests. But there .... a shadow over Tony's new-found happiness, for he .... that one day George's rightful owner .... When the inevitable ...., though, things .... out rather unexpectedly both for Tony and for George.

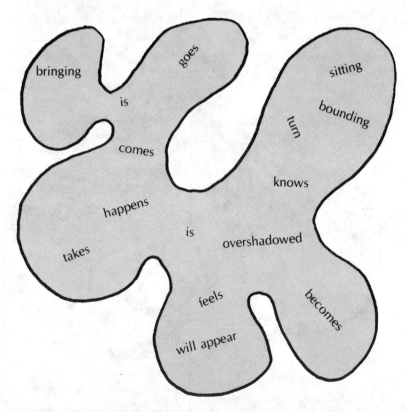

MIDNITE
the story of a wild colonial boy

RANDOLPH STOW

4. A Hold-Up

Midnite is a kind-hearted, reluctant and not-so-bright bushranger, who has to be helped in his humorous adventures by his confederate Khat, a very determined Siamese cat. In this passage, our hero is attempting not very successfully to rob a stage coach.

When they were about twenty miles from the town, and were going up a very steep hill, a voice called out of the bush: 'Stand and deliver! Your money or your lives!'

'Who said that?' demanded the Judge, sticking his red face out of the coach window.

'A bushranger, Your Honour,' said Trooper O'Grady. 'That is what they always say.'

'Well, shoot him,' said the Judge, crossly.

'You shoot him, sir,' said the trooper. 'My pistols are inside the coach with you.'

'Throw the pistols to me,' snarled the voice in the bush, 'or you are a dead man.'

'That's curious,' murmured Trooper O'Grady. 'The voice has a Siamese accent.'

'Don't make personal remarks,' snapped Khat (for of course it was Khat). 'Stand with your hands above your heads, and if I catch anyone not shivering in his shoes, he's in trouble.'

Trooper O'Grady and the driver put up their hands, while Judge Pepper still stared from the coach. From being a red-faced shiny man he had turned into a white-faced shiny man.

'Throw me the pistols, Judge Pepper,' called Khat, 'or I'll tear out your heart and eat it.'

'No, no,' cried Judge Pepper, trembling, as he threw the pistols into the bush. 'Have pity on me. I have a great-aunt and eleven cousins in Wagga Wagga.'

'Let them beware,' said Khat, with a bloodcurdling laugh. 'Now, Judge Pepper, get out of the coach, and stand beside Trooper O'Grady with your hands up.'

The Judge got out as he was told, though his knees were shaking so much that he could hardly walk, and he stood in a line with Trooper O'Grady and the driver.

'Our leader is coming to rob you,' said Khat. 'If any one of you moves, he is a dead man.'

'You've already said that,' remarked Trooper O'Grady.

'Keep a civil tongue in your head, O'Grady,' snarled Khat, 'or I will nail it to a tree.'

Suddenly there was a thunderous crash, and out of the thick bush bounded a tall and noble-minded horse, with a long-legged bushranger on his back. Midnite dismounted, and strode towards Judge Pepper. He had a red handkerchief over his face, hiding everything except his blue eyes, and he held one of Trooper O'Grady's pistols in his right hand.

'Your money or your life?' he asked Judge Pepper, rather shyly.

'Oh, my money,' said the Judge, shaking from head to foot, 'of course.'

'Give me your purse, then,' said the bushranger.

'And your watch and chain,' called Khat from the bush.

'And your watch and chain,' repeated the bushranger, going red in the tops of his ears.

The Judge pulled out his fat purse and his watch, and gave them to the bushranger, who put them carefully in the pocket of his coat.

The driver, meanwhile, had been counting the loose change that he kept in his trousers pocket, and he said to the bushranger: 'Four and twopence. Is that any use to you, mate?'

'Oh, no,' said the bushranger, embarrassed. 'No, you keep it.'

'You can have it, mate,' said the driver, 'if you need it.'

'Oh no, please,' said the bushranger, 'you have it. I've got rather a lot of money, as a matter of fact.'

'I wouldn't want to leave you short,' said the driver.

'Hold your tongue,' Khat called to the driver, 'or we'll cut your head off and send it to your mother.'

'If that's the way you feel about it, mate,' said the driver, shrugging his shoulders.

RANDOLPH STOW, *Midnite*

A Hold-Up 25

1. Reading for Meaning

(a) What is the meaning of 'stand and deliver'?
(b) How does the Judge first react to the bushranger's demand?
(c) Why couldn't Trooper O'Grady shoot the bushranger?
(d) What does 'Have pity on me. I have a great-aunt and eleven cousins in Wagga Wagga,' reveal about the Judge's character?
(e) What evidence can you find to show that Midnite was an inexperienced bushranger?
(f) What evidence can you find to show that Midnite is a kind person?
(g) What are your feelings about Khat?
(h) What did the story tell you about the physical appearance of Midnite?
(i) What happens in the story that makes you feel it is not true to life?
(j) What is the meaning of the following words?
(You may like to use your back-of-the-book dictionary to help you.)
   (i) bloodcurdling   (ii) civil
   (iii) snarled   (iv) shrugged

2. Finding New Words

Replace the writer's words in heavy print with words of your own that have similar meanings.

(a) If I catch anyone not **shivering in his shoes** he's in trouble.
(b) Have **pity** on me.
(c) Keep a **civil** tongue in your head, O'Grady.
(d) The Judge got out as he was **told,** though his knees were **shaking** so much that he could **hardly** walk.
(e) 'You can have it, **mate,'** **said** the driver.
(f) He had a red handkerchief over his face, **hiding** everything except his blue eyes.
(g) 'Oh, my money,' said the Judge, shaking **from head to foot,** **'of course.'**
(h) 'That's **curious,'** **murmured** Trooper O'Grady.

3. Who, Whom, Whose, Which, That

Use your knowledge of the story to complete these sentences.
(a) Trooper O'Grady, whose ...., was told by the Judge to shoot the bushranger.
(b) Judge Pepper, who ...., threw the pistols into the bush.
(c) Midnite put into his pocket the fat purse and watch which ....
(d) Out of the thick bush bounded a tall and noble-minded horse, which ....
(e) Midnite, who .... , held one of Trooper O'Grady's pistols in his right hand.
(f) The driver had been counting the loose change that ....
(g) Midnite refused the money which ....
(h) The driver, whom Khat ...., shrugged his shoulders.

4. Write Down the Nouns

Write down the nouns which come from each of the following words from the story. The first one has been done for you.

	WORD	NOUN
	strode	stride
(a)	carefully	
(b)	deliver	
(c)	demanded	
(d)	red	
(e)	crossly	
(f)	shoot	
(g)	snarled	
(h)	shiny	
(i)	cried	
(j)	embarrassed	
(k)	civil	
(l)	loose	
(m)	shyly	
(n)	repeated	
(o)	said	

5. Complete the Sentences

Using your knowledge of the story, complete the sentences.
(a) Judge Pepper asked for pity, because ....
(b) Midnite dismounted after ....
(c) The Judge got out of the coach although ....
(d) Khat said that if Judge Pepper .... he would be killed.
(e) Khat gave instructions while ....
(f) Midnite told the driver to keep the four and twopence because ....

6. Use the Correct Word

Write down the sentences, inserting in the blank spaces the correct form of the words in brackets.

(a) The driver merely .... his shoulders. [shrugging].
(b) Midnite's .... was not that of a normal bushranger. [personal].
(c) Khat took .... to the driver's helpfulness. [except].
(d) The hold-up was a .... event. [remark].
(e) Trooper O'Grady showed .... about Khat's voice. [curious].
(f) The driver proved .... to Khat. [trouble].
(g) The Judge in many ways was a man to be .... [pity].
(h) The Judge was not a very .... man. [honour].

7. Attaching the Phrases

A phrase is a group of words which does not have a verb with a subject. Complete the sentences by attaching the correct phrases.

	SENTENCE	PHRASE
(a)	Keep a civil tongue	from the town
(b)	The Judge was shaking	above your heads
(c)	Judge Pepper threw the pistols	over his face
(d)	They were about twenty miles	in your head
(e)	Judge Pepper still stared	into the bush
(f)	A bushranger strode	in his right hand
(g)	He had a red handkerchief	to Judge Pepper
(h)	He held one of Trooper O'Grady's pistols	from the coach
(i)	Stand with your hands	from head to foot

8. Variation of Words for 'Said'

The writer has used other words instead of 'said'. See whether you can find them using the clues.

(a) c _ _ _ _ _
(b) a _ _ _ _
(c) d _ _ _ _ _ _ _
(d) r _ _ _ _ _ _ _
(e) s _ _ _ _ _ _
(f) m _ _ _ _ _ _ _
(g) s _ _ p _ _ _

5. Some Pig!

Fern doesn't know it but Wilbur, her pet pig, is due to be turned into smoked bacon and ham. However, Charlotte the spider, who is Wilbur's friend, has a plan. She thinks, 'The way to save Wilbur's life is to play a trick on Zuckerman'. So, here's the trick she plays on Zuckerman, the farmer:

On foggy mornings, Charlotte's web was truly a thing of beauty. This morning each thin strand was decorated with dozens of tiny beads of water. The web glistened in the light and made a pattern of loveliness and mystery, like a delicate veil. Even Lurvy, who wasn't particularly interested in beauty, noticed the web when he came with the pig's breakfast. He noted how clearly it showed up and he noted how big and carefully built it was. And then he took another look and he saw something that made him set his pail down. There, in the centre of the web, neatly woven in block letters, was a message. It said:

SOME PIG!

Lurvy felt weak. He brushed his hand across his eyes and stared harder at Charlotte's web.

'I'm seeing things,' he whispered. He dropped to his knees and uttered a short prayer. Then, forgetting all about Wilbur's breakfast, he walked back to the house and called Mr Zuckerman.

'I think you'd better come down to the pigpen,' he said.

'What's the trouble?' asked Mr Zuckerman. 'Anything wrong with the pig?'

'No — not exactly,' said Lurvy. 'Come and see for yourself.'

The two men walked silently down to Wilbur's yard. Lurvy pointed to the spider's web. 'Do you see what I see?' he asked.

Zuckerman stared at the writing on the web. Then he murmured the words 'Some Pig'. Then he looked at Lurvy. Then they both began to tremble. Charlotte, sleepy after her night's exertions, smiled as she watched. Wilbur came and stood directly under the web.

'Some pig!' muttered Lurvy in a low voice.

'Some pig!' whispered Mr Zuckerman. They stared and stared for a long time at Wilbur. Then they stared at Charlotte.

'You don't suppose that that spider . . .' began Mr Zuckerman — but he shook his head and didn't finish the sentence. Instead, he walked solemnly back up to the house and spoke to his wife. 'Edith, something has happened,' he said, in a weak voice. He went into the living-room and sat down, and Mrs Zuckerman followed.

'I've got something to tell you, Edith,' he said. 'You better sit down.'

Mrs Zuckerman sank into a chair. She looked pale and frightened.

'Edith,' he said, trying to keep his voice steady, 'I think you had best be told that we have a very unusual pig.'

E. B. WHITE, *Charlotte's Web*

1. Reading for Meaning

(a) Why was Charlotte's web particularly beautiful on *foggy* mornings?
(b) The web is compared to something else. What is it?
(c) What errand is Lurvy on when we first meet him?
(d) He notes three things about the web — and then a fourth! What are they?
(e) 'Lurvy felt weak.' Why?
(f) What is the first thing that Lurvy does after he thinks he's seeing things?
(g) Why do you think Charlotte smiles as she watches the men tremble under the web?
(h) It is essential that Wilbur stand as near as possible to the web. What does this do for him?
(i) Can you suggest any reason for Mr Zuckerman's refusal to believe a spider 'wrote' the message?
(j) How does Mr Zuckerman describe Wilbur to Mrs Zuckerman?

2. Head Spinners

Words about Charlotte and Wilbur are woven into the web. The trouble is that the letters have become twisted around a little. Straighten them out and place them in the boxes (draw these in your workbook) using the clues. Note the example.

Some Pig! 33

Web words: YESTRYM, ANULUSU, NEGPIP, BEW, PARNTET, TEXIRONSE, GIP, DIPSER, SAMEGES, DRANTS, TORDEDACE

	CLUES	BOXES
(a)	Wilbur	P I G
(b)	Charlotte's . . .	W _ _
(c)	A part of the web	S _ _ _ _
(d)	Charlotte herself	S _ _ _ _ _
(e)	Where Wilbur resides	P _ _ _ _
(f)	Uncommon	U _ _ _ _ _
(g)	A certain shape	P _ _ _ _ _
(h)	SOME PIG is a . . .	M _ _ _ _ _
(i)	Strangeness and secrecy	M _ _ _ _ _
(j)	Efforts	E _ _ _ _ _ _
(k)	Beautified	D _ _ _ _ _ _

3. Tail Endings

The same word may take on different endings depending on how it is being used in a sentence.

It was a real mystery

They all agreed it was a myster*ious* happening.

Here are words from the passage that need tailing off with endings. Notice that you only get the basic part of each word. So try to fit each basic part to its proper endings. Note the example.

BASIC PARTS		
beaut	lov	weak
silen	fright	vo
decorat	happen	forget
care	centr	troubl
neat		

TAIL ENDINGS					
(a)	weak ness weak ly	(f)	ful fully	(k)	liness ly e
(b)	ice cal	(g)	ness ly	(l)	ce t tly
(c)	e al ally ed	(h)	ing ed	(m)	e ed ion
(d)	ting ful fulness	(i)	ful fully en ened ening		
(e)	y iful ifully ify	(j)	e esome ing ed		

4. Verb Threesomes

There are plenty of verbs — action words — helping out Charlotte, Wilbur and the Zuckermans in the passage.

Using the stems of passage verbs fill in the past tense and past participle columns. Fill them in using the 'I saw', 'I have seen' model given. But be careful — sometimes the past tense and the past participle of a verb are different; sometimes they are the same. Test and see!

	VERB STEM to . . .	PAST TENSE I . . .	PAST PARTICIPLE I have . . .
	see	I **saw**	I have **seen**
(a)	forget		
(b)	write		
(c)	tremble		
(d)	stand		
(e)	try		
(f)	begin		
(g)	be		
(h)	sit		
(i)	**make**		
(j)	come		
(k)	have		
(l)	feel		
(m)	weave		
(n)	show		
(o)	shake		
(p)	speak		
(q)	sink		

5. Some Pig!

Statements (Wilbur is a pig.)
Questions (Who's Charlotte?)
Exclamations (Some Pig!)
all occur in the passage.

Rewrite the following expressions in your workbook, giving the statements a full stop [.], the questions a question mark [?] and the exclamations an exclamation mark [!].

(a) Charlotte's full name was Charlotte A. Cavatica
(b) Anything wrong with the pig
(c) Wow
(d) She looked pale and frightened
(e) Good on you, Charlotte
(f) What's the trouble
(g) Look at that
(h) Do you see what I see
(i) They stared at Charlotte
(j) Some spider
(k) Did the spider do it
(l) They both began to tremble
(m) Hooray for Charlotte
(n) He shook his head
(o) Where's Wilbur
(p) Lurvy felt weak
(q) How was it done
(r) What a pig

6. Weaving in Shades of Meaning

'Zuckerman **stared** at the writing on the web.'
'Lurvy **walked** back to the house and called Mr Zuckerman.'
'Stared' and 'walked' are words dealing with particular uses of the eyes and legs. But, suppose you want to weave in other shades of meaning? There's a range of words available. Try this exercise and see for yourself . . .

On the left are expressions dealing with particular ways of using the eyes and legs. On the right are 'shades-of-meaning' words that match up with the expressions. Match up words and expressions in your workbook. Note the example.

	EXPRESSIONS	SHADES OF MEANING WORDS
(a)	a long, hard, even rude look	sprint
(b)	to take long steps	march
(c)	an angry look	hobble
(d)	a short, fast dash	hurry
(e)	follow print	stride
(f)	move in time to music	stroll
(g)	a long look around	stare
(h)	a duck-like walk	glimpse
(i)	to look with the idea of making an object clearer	hike
(j)	a pleasant, unhurried walk	squint
(k)	to walk with speed	dawdle
(l)	a look into the light	waddle
(m)	to walk in step	survey
(n)	a quick sighting	glare
(o)	the kind of walk that goes with sore feet	read
(p)	to examine very carefully, looking for faults	focus
(q)	to walk in the bush with a rucksack	dance
(r)	a time-wasting walk	scrutinize

7. Stranded

Some of the little words that are so important in linking other words and expressions have been stranded in a corner of the frame below.

Rewrite the words and expressions in the frame below, putting in the words from the spider web. One example has been done for you.

EXAMPLE:

(a) See *for* yourself.

(b) Decorated .... dozens .... tiny beads .... water.
(c) Lurvy pointed .... the spider's web.
(d) Interested .... beauty.
(e) He looked .... Lurvy.
(f) Mr Zuckerman sank .... a chair.
(g) He spoke .... his wife.
(h) Sleepy .... her night's exertions.
(i) He came .... the pig's breakfast.
(j) Wilbur stood directly .... the web.

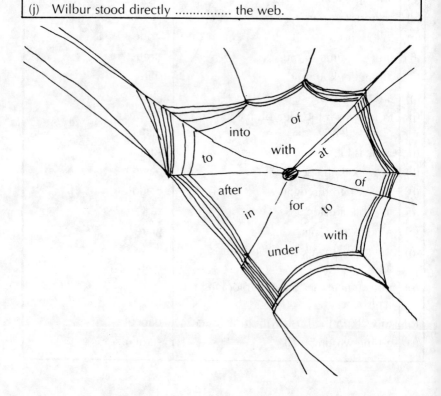

8. Nouns from the Pigpen

Replace important, missing nouns from the summary with fitting nouns from the pigpen! Rewrite the passage in your workbook including the missing nouns as you go.

Charlotte's Web

This is the .... of a little .... named .... who loved a little .... named ...., and of how Wilbur's dear friend, Charlotte A. Cavatica, a beautiful grey ...., saved Wilbur from the usual fate of nice fat .... by a wonderfully clever .... which no one else could have possibly thought of.

There are a lot of other interesting .... on Mr Zuckerman's ....; notably a cynical grey .... called Templeton and a most irresponsible goose, both of whom help to make Wilbur the most famous pig in the ....

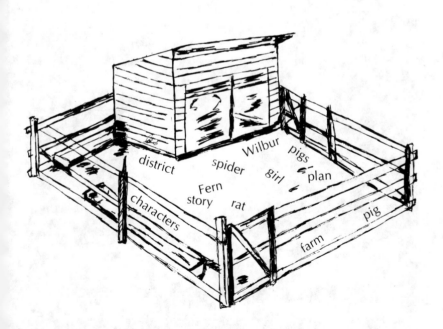

6. The Waterspout

Snook Pascoe's father thought the boy would never amount to much, never make a fisherman. Even Snook wondered — until the day he had to succeed.

Instantly an amazing thing happened. A great column of water rose up out of the sea, thrust itself head and shoulders into the black fury of the vortex above and began moving across the sea like a waltzing mountain. The shrieking wind inside the funnel had done its most spectacular work: its speed had spun a vacuum in the air, and sucked the pillar of water into it like liquid up a straw.

The hiss of the wind was now joined by the crash of tearing water. Snook heard it and looked up. For a second he didn't comprehend what he saw: the black funnel, a mile high, hanging above him, the obelisk of water standing on the ocean only a hundred yards away, the sibilant shriek that was unlike any sound he'd ever heard on earth — all these momentarily carried no meaning.

But only momentarily. Then he dropped the chumming scoop, leapt from the bait tank to the deck and screamed at the others. 'A waterspout! Look out! A waterspout! A waterspout!' Years later he could see again in his mind's eye the terrible events of the next three seconds: the blanched faces of the four men as they looked up in fear and surprise like animals taken unawares; their feverish unbuckling of safety belts and desperate clambering out of the racks to escape the destruction roaring down on them; the bull-like bellow of his father as he leapt across the deck for the wheel-house. And then for a long time, nothing that could be remembered clearly at all.

There was a fantastic screaming in his ears as the black wall bore down and engulfed them. He was lifted up and hurled away like straw. Kaleidoscopic pictures flashed before him, so it seemed — the heavy steel racks and one of the white dinghies spiralling high above him, the three polers from the stern pin-wheeling away in the air ten feet beyond the ship, the bait-tank wrenched out and tossed away like crumpled paper. For a second he could have sworn that the ship was in the air, borne aloft bodily and spun round like a white ball on a jet of water. Disintegrating timbers flew past him — bits of board, panels of glass and wood from the wheel-hours, stanchions and rails, pieces of dinghy, poles, lines, and ropes. Then he felt himself flung down the open hatch onto the brine tanks below. Something struck him sickeningly across the small of the back and a piece of steel raked his arm. Hundreds of tons of water seemed to crash down on the ship. She lurched crazily, and Snook knew she was gone; *Blue Fin* was joining *Dog Star* and he wondered vaguely whether Snitch and Sam would be waiting for him there. And all the rest of the phantom fleet that had been spirited away for ever.

COLIN THIELE, *Blue Fin*

1. Reading for Meaning

(a) What job did Snook carry out on the boat?
   (i) Steering the boat
   (ii) Working a fishing pole
   (iii) Chumming, i.e. dropping live bait into the sea to attract the tuna
(b) How many men, including Snook's father, were working the fishing poles catching tuna?
(c) Why were the polers taken unawares by the waterspout?
(d) What was the 'most spectacular work' of the shrieking wind?
(e) When the waterspout started, what other sound was added to the hiss of the wind?
(f) Explain why the first reaction of Snook's dad was to rush for the wheel-house.
(g) Do you think that Snook was lucky to have survived? Why?
(h) Find one sentence in the third paragraph which indicates to you that Snook was going to survive this incident.
(i) What brief impressions about the ship did Snook have after the waterspout hit?
(j) From the final sentence, what might you be able to conclude about 'Dog Star' and Snitch and Sam?

2. Snook Experiences the Tornado

Below is a list of events experienced by Snook when the waterspout hit. Separate the events into three categories — sights, sounds and feelings. One has been done to give you the idea!

SIGHTS	SOUNDS	FEELINGS
the black funnel		

the hiss of the wind
the black funnel
the blanched faces of the polers
the bellow of his father
something hitting him in the back
fantastic screaming
disintegrating timbers flying past
being flung down the hatch
the crash of tearing water
the obelisk of water
the polers' feverish unbuckling of safety belts
being lifted up and hurled away
the white dinghies spiralling above
a piece of steel raking his arm

3. Matching Words and Meanings

Match each word in the list below, with its correct meaning from the jumbled meanings column. Use the back-of-the-book dictionary if you need help!

	WORD	MEANING
(a)	vortex	hissing; sounded with a hiss (like the sound 's')
(b)	comprehend	in the air; up above
(c)	unawares	space entirely devoid of matter or air
(d)	obelisk	a spinning tunnel
(e)	feverish	carried
(f)	sibilant	pale; white in colour
(g)	brine	understand; make sense of
(h)	aloft	swamped; buried; swallowed up
(i)	vacuum	unexpectedly; by surprise
(j)	blanched	excited
(k)	engulfed	breaking up; falling to pieces
(l)	borne	salt water
(m)	disintegrating	a tapering shape; usually stone object which narrows towards the top

4. Tuna-Fishing Terms

Select the appropriate terms from the panel to complete each of the sentences. Use each term only once.

> Chumming wheel-house lure rippler metal traces bait-tank bow echo-sounder single-polers after-deck

(a) He seemed to concentrate all his attention on the jiggling .... until a tuna bit.

(b) With all the fish lying on it, the .... was a shambles.

(c) 'Let's hope they're ....,' Snook's father said, 'otherwise, I'll have to give Con a hand'.

The Waterspout

(d) 'Keep ....,' the skipper called. 'They may start biting any minute now.'
(e) The .... of the *Blue Fin* cut through the heavy seas with ease.
(f) As the polers hauled each fish aboard the .... twanged with the tension on them.
(g) Snook dug his net into the .... and brought up four or five pounds of struggling chow.
(h) Snook watched the .... in awe as the sea floor suddenly plunged downwards.
(i) Snook's father shouted instructions from the .... where he was steering.
(j) 'I see 'em' said Snook's father, staring at the choppy surface ahead of the tuna. 'Look's a good ....'

5. 'Sound' Words

Snook hears the 'shrieking' and the 'hiss' of the wind and the 'crash' of the water. There are many words like this in our language — words which actually sound like the thing they are describing.

Find suitable 'sound' words for the following phrases. Use a different word each time.

(a) the .... of car tyres
(b) the .... of cymbals
(c) the .... of pigs at feeding time
(d) the .... of hoof beats
(e) the .... of a leaking tap
(f) the .... of a boxer hitting his opponent
(g) the .... of tiny bells
(h) the .... of a flock of sparrows
(i) the .... of a lion
(j) the .... of tiny feet
(k) the .... of an injured person
(l) the .... of an overtired child

6. Scope Words

'Kaleidoscopic pictures flashed before him . . .'

A kaleidoscope is a tube in which are seen brightly coloured pieces of glass which change their pattern as the tube is rotated. In this sentence 'kaleidoscopic' means 'changing objects and colours'.

All words ending in *'scope'* have something to do with what is seen, or examined.

Match the *'scope'* words with their correct meanings. Use the dictionary to check any you are unsure of. The first letter of each one is given after its meaning, to help you.

(a) telescope (b) microscope (c) gyroscope (d) spectroscope (e) periscope (f) epidiascope (g) horoscope (h) stethoscope (i) stereoscope (j) laryngoscope

(a) an instrument for viewing two photos of the same view or object, taken from slightly different angles [S]; (b) an instrument for seeing over long distances [T]; (c) an instrument for listening to the heart [S]; (d) a kind of overhead projector which projects images of opaque *and* transparent objects [E]; (e) an observation of the sky and planets at a certain time [H]; (f) an instrument dealing with the properties of rotation or spin [G]; (g) an instrument which magnifies small objects [M]; (h) an instrument for examining the spectra of rays [S]; (i) a mirror apparatus for examining a person's larynx [L]; (j) an instrument enabling someone in a submerged position to see above the water [P].

WORD	MEANING
(a)	....
(b)	....
(c)	....
(d)	....
(e)	....
(f)	....
(g)	....
(h)	....
(i)	....
(j)	....

7. Change-A-Word

Each of the words below is taken from the passage. By following the clues and shuffling the order of the letters you can change each word into a new word. The first one is done to give you the idea, and the first letter of each is provided.

(a) *Leapt* becomes the leaf of a flower   [Petal]
(b) *Straw* becomes tiny growths on a person's hands   [W]
(c) *Yards* becomes carts pulled by horses   [D]
(d) *Bore* becomes an article of clothing   [R]
(e) *Time* becomes a tiny child   [M]
(f) *Stern* becomes what tenants pay   [R]
(g) *Ropes* becomes tiny openings in the skin   [P]
(h) *Poles* becomes a gradient or inclination   [S]
(i) *Aloft* becomes to stay up in water   [F]
(j) *Earth* becomes a major organ of the body   [H]

7. A Crazy Conversation

*'When I woke up this morning I found I'd turned into my mother.'
This is the funny and fast-moving story of how thirteen-year-old
Annabel Andrews copes with the problems of being her own mother for
a day.*

I found a bowl of leftover macaroni in the fridge and I was just about to sit down and watch 'The Little Rascals' when the doorbell rang. Not expecting anybody and not wishing to be robbed on this, the most splendid day of my life, I peeked through the burglar hole . . . and almost fainted dead away. On the other side of the door stood Boris Harris!

Boris Harris is fourteen, he has chestnut hair and hazel eyes. I don't know how tall he is but it's a good three inches more than I am, and whatever he weighs is just perfect. He lives in our building, he is beautiful, and I love him.

'And he is standing outside our door right this minute holding a spaghetti sieve, and how am I going to handle the situation?' I asked myself. 'With charm and sophistication,' I answered myself, and with that I hid the bowl of macaroni in a waste-basket, and flung open the door.

'Why, good morning, *Boris*!' I said. 'What a lovely surprise!'

'I cabe to returd your collader,' said Boris.

'That's very sweet of you,' I said.

'It was by buther's idea because it was by buther who borrowed it,' said Boris.

'Ah well, yes, I see what you mean,' I said, 'but in any case, why don't you come in for a minute. The hall is no place to be standing in a negligee, don't you agree?.

'Doh. I guess dot,' said Boris, stepping over the threshold (What *took* him so long?), 'but I cad ohdly stay a biddit — by buther is expecting be hobe.'

'Poor Boris, that's a perfectly dreadful cold you've got there. Do you ever take Vitamin C? Let me get you some Vitamin C.'

'Please dohd bother, Brs Andrews, I dohd . . .'

'It's no bother at all,' I shouted over my shoulder as I galloped to the kitchen. 'Why don't you sit down in the living room and make yourself comfortable? I'm coming right back.'

I did come right back, but it took me a minute to find him because, dear God, do you know where he was? Standing in the doorway of my Annabel's room, wide-eyed and slack-jawed. Slack-jawed could be due to the cold, but wide-eyed, I'm afraid, was due to something else.

'Who lives *there*?' he said, wrinkling his adorable red nose.

'My son Ben,' I said, closing the door firmly.

'With a cadopy bed ad a *doll* house?'

'Yes, with a canopy bed and a dollhouse,' I said. 'My son is a very peculiar little boy.'

'I'll say,' agreed Boris. 'He is also a slob.'

MARY RODGERS, *Freaky Friday*

1. Reading for Meaning

(a) What is it that Annabel does not wish to be 'robbed' of?

(b) What is it about Boris Harris that almost causes Annabel to faint when she sees him outside the door?

(c) Outline three descriptive features of Boris Harris.

(d) 'Whatever he weighs is just perfect.' According to whose judgement is Boris's weight just perfect?

(e) Where does Annabel hide the bowl of macaroni before she lets Boris in?

(f) Why is Boris's speech so strange?

(g) Why did Annabel have some trouble spotting Boris again when she returned to the room?

(h) 'With a cadopy bed and a *doll* house?' Explain why the writer has put the word 'doll' in italics in this case.

(i) Give an explanation for Annabel's lie when she says that it is Ben's room.

(j) Why does Boris conclude that Ben is a slob?

2. Annabel — the Mixture

When a person wakes up and finds she has become her mother, it isn't easy to adjust! Some of Annabel's words and actions still seem to fit the thirteen-year-old, and some seem to fit Mrs Andrews — all mixed up in Annabel!

Below is a list of word groups, some describing actions. Separate them into two columns headed THE THIRTEEN-YEAR-OLD and THE ADULT.

(a) flung open the door
(b) 'My son, Ben'
(c) 'with charm and sophistication,' I answered myself
(d) my son is a very peculiar little boy
(e) almost fainted dead away
(f) I galloped into the kitchen
(g) 'Why don't you sit down in the living room and make yourself comfortable?'
(h) he is beautiful, and I love him
(i) 'Whatever he weighs is just perfect'
(j) 'That's very sweet of you'
(k) I shouted over my shoulder

3. Freaky Spelling

Each of the following words from the passage has been spelt in three different ways in the lists below. Only one spelling is correct. Identify the correctly-spelt word in each case, and use it in a sentence.

(a)	burgular	burgler	burglar
(b)	spahgetti	spaghetti	spagheti
(c)	foreteen	fourteen	forteen
(d)	vitammin	vitemin	vitamin
(e)	sophistication	sophistacation	sophistikation
(f)	peculier	peculiar	peculair
(g)	macarroni	macaroni	maccaroni
(h)	threshold	thresold	threhsold
(i)	seive	sievie	sieve

4. What Word is Meant by . . .?

Boris has a cold in the nose, so some words are difficult for him to pronounce properly. To check your understanding of what he says in the passage, write alongside each of his words below, the word that he really means. The first one is done for you.

WHAT BORIS SAYS	WHAT BORIS MEANS
cabe	came
returd	....
collader	....
buther	....
by	....
doh	....
dot	....
cad	....
ohdly	....
biddit	....
expectig	....
be	....
hobe	....
dohd	....
ad	....

5. Words and Meanings

Find words from the extract which have the same meaning as the following. The first letter of each word is given and the first one is done for you to give you the idea.

	MEANING	WORD
	scamps; naughty children	Rascals
(a)	Set of circumstances	S................
(b)	Regarded with the utmost affection and respect	A................
(c)	Peeped, peered	P................
(d)	An item of night attire	N................
(e)	Such as to promote content and ease	C................
(f)	Putting furrow-like creases in a surface	W................
(g)	Deep reddish-brown	C................
(h)	Attractiveness; indefinable power of delighting	C................
(i)	Looking forward to; regarding as likely	E................

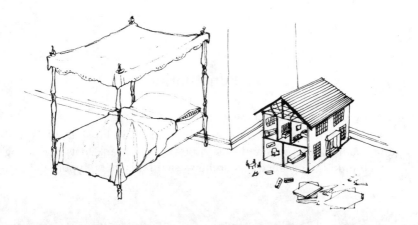

54 Word Skills One

6. Annabel Words

Below is a list of 'Annabel' words — the sort that thirteen-year-old Annabel Andrews would use!

Beneath the list is a passage written in fairly normal English. Your task is to re-write the passage, substituting an 'Annabel' word from the list for each of the words in italics. Use each list word, or group, only once.

    mucking around
    kids
    fabulous
    fed up
    lover boy
    crazy
    gooey
    the fink
    dumb face
    lousy
    boob tube
    grimy goodies

'One thing that I remembered just in time was to make the *children's* lunches. *Ben* was playing but I became *tired* so I told him to stop the *terrible* din and take all his *dirty clothes* to the laundry. Annabel was sitting in front of the *TV* eating some *soft* marshmallows. I told her to get ready for school, and saw her pull a *silly face* when she thought I'd turned away. *The foolish child*! Anyway, I was ready for such an *enjoyable* day, it would have been *foolish* of me to react. I sent them off to school and settled down.'

7. Punctuation

Correctly punctuate the following passage.

  shes much nicer now than she used to be I said Im sure she is said boris amiably but mrs andrews to be perfectly frank thats not saying much thud long silence mrs andrews said boris its not your fault that annabel is the way she is

8. Verb and Object Match-up

Match the verbs with the objects they take in the passage.

	VERB	OBJECT
(a)	make	Vitamin C
(b)	found	the bowl
(c)	is expecting	the door
(d)	take	spaghetti sieve
(e)	wrinkling	anybody
(f)	is (also)	your collader
(g)	closing	adorable red nose
(h)	holding	a bowl
(i)	expecting	yourself
(j)	to returd	be
(k)	hid	a slob

Island of the BLUE DOLPHINS

Scott O'Dell

A Newbery Award Winner

8. The Devilfish

Karana is a twelve-year-old Indian girl, who is telling the story of her adventures and hardships on a desolate island off the coast of California. Her only companion is her dog, Rontu.

The giant slid up on the sand. He lay with his arms spread out, partly in the water, and I thought he was dead. Then I saw his eyes moving. Before I could shout a warning, Rontu had rushed forward and seized him. But the devilfish was too heavy to lift or shake. As Rontu's jaws sought another hold, three of the many arms wound themselves around his neck.

Devilfish are only dangerous when in the water where they can fasten themselves to you with their long arms. These arms have rows of suckers underneath them and they can drag you under and hold you there until you drown. But even on land the devilfish can injure you, for he is strong and does not die quickly.

The giant was flailing his arms, struggling to get back into the water. Little by little he was dragging Rontu with him. I could no longer use the string because it was wound around Rontu's legs.

The whalebone knife I used for prying abalones from the rocks was tied to a thong at my waist. The blade was thick at the point but had a sharp edge. I dropped the coils of string and unfastened the knife as I ran.

I ran past the devilfish and got between him and the deep water. So many of his arms were flailing that it was useless to cut any one of them. One struck me on the leg and burned like a whip. Another, which Rontu had chewed off, lay wriggling at the edge of the water, as if it were looking for something to fasten on to.

The head rose out of the twisting arms like a giant stalk. The gold eyes with their black rims were fixed on me. Above the sounds of the waves and the water splashing and Rontu's barking, I could hear the snapping of his beak, which was sharper than the knife I held in my hand.

I drove the knife down into his body and as I did this I was suddenly covered, or so it seemed, with a countless number of leeches, sucking at my skin. Fortunately one hand was free, the hand that held the knife, and again and again I struck down through the tough hide. The suckers, which were fastened to me and pained greatly, lessened their hold. Slowly the arms stopped moving and then grew limp.

I tried to drag the devilfish out of the water, but my strength was gone. I did not even go back to the reef for my canoe, though I did take the shaft and the head of the spear, which had cost me much labour, and the sinew line.

It was night before Rontu and I got back to the house.

Rontu had a gash on his nose from the giant's beak, and I had many cuts and bruises. I saw two more giant devilfish along the reef that summer, but I did not try to spear them.

SCOTT O'DELL, *Island of the Blue Dolphins*

1. Reading for Meaning

(a) How did Karana (the girl in the story) know that the devilfish was not dead?
(b) Why is a devilfish particularly dangerous in the water?
(c) Why is the devilfish on land still capable of causing injury?
(d) Why did it seem as if Rontu was losing the fight with the devilfish?
(e) Why did Karana get between the devilfish and the deep water?
(f) Why didn't Karana keep trying to cut off the arms of the devilfish?
(g) What happened when Karana first drove her knife into the devilfish's body?
(h) Why was Karana unable to drag the devilfish out of the water?
(i) Why do you think Karana did not try to spear the two other giant devilfish she saw along the reef that summer?
(j) What is the meaning of these words used in the passage?
    (a) sought
    (b) prying
    (c) thong
    (d) limp
(You may like to consult your back-of-the-book dictionary to help you.)

2. In Your Own Words

Rewrite each of the following sentences using words of your own that are similar in meaning to the words in heavy print.

(a) Before I could **shout** a warning, Rontu had rushed forward and **seized** him.
(b) **Little by little**, he was dragging Rontu with him.
(c) Devilfish are only **dangerous** when in the water where they can **fasten** themselves to you with their long arms.
(d) He lay with his **arms** spread out, partly in the water, and I **thought** he was dead.
(e) So many of his arms were flailing that it was **useless** to **cut** any one of them.
(f) **Fortunately** one hand was **free**, the hand that held the knife, and again and again I struck down through the tough hide.
(g) The suckers, which were fastened to me and **pained greatly**, lessened their **hold**.
(h) I **tried** to drag the **devilfish** out of the water, but **my strength was gone**.

3. Putting Sentences Back Together

Put each of these sentences from the story back together. A good approach is to find the verbs first, then the subjects of the verbs and work from there.

(a) giant of the arms stalk the like a out rose twisting head
(b) house it the was to night back before got Rontu I and
(c) stopped grew and limp slowly then the moving arms
(d) struck burned leg whip on one me the a and like
(e) water past him and between ran got I the the and deep devilfish
(f) string ran dropped the and of I coils unfastened as knife I the

4. Correct the Sentences

Write down the sentences, selecting the correct word from the brackets.

(a) As I [drive/drove] the knife down into his body I seemed to be covered with countless leeches, sucking at my skin.
(b) It [is/was] difficult to kill the devilfish because it had [that/so] many arms.
(c) Fortunately one of my hands [were/was] free and I [struck/strike] down through the tough hide.
(d) I ran [past/passed] the devilfish and got between [he/him] and the deep water.
(e) So many of his arms [was/were] flailing that it [were/was] useless to cut any [ones/one] of them.
(f) I [saw/seen] two more giant devilfish, but I did not try to spear [they/them].
(g) One of the arms of the devilfish [was/were] seen wriggling on the beach.
(h) Rontu had rushed forward [quickly/quick].
(i) The devilfish was one of the [uglier/ugliest] creatures that Rontu had even [saw/seen].
(j) The devilfish could [of/have] killed Rontu and Karana.

5. Finding Subjects

Using your knowledge of the story, insert **subjects** in these sentences.

(a) Its .... was sharper than the knife.
(b) Many .... wound themselves around Rontu's neck.
(c) .... are underneath the devilfish's arms.
(d) A .... was tied to a thong at my waist.
(e) .... had rushed forward and seized the devilfish.
(f) The .... rose out of the twisting arms like a giant stalk.
(g) The .... had a sharp edge.
(h) .... had many cuts and bruises.
(i) The .... of the devilfish was very tough.
(j) The .... of the devilfish were fixed on me.

6. Clues

Using the clues, find the missing words from the story.

(a) The sound of a dog   b.....
(b) The past tense of seek   s.....
(c) This word means 'very many'   c.....
(d) These suck blood out of you   l.....
(e) The opposite to safe   d.....
(f) A deep cut   g.....
(g) A noise made by striking water in water   s.....
(h) An edible shellfish   m.....
(i) A piece of tough tissue   s.....
(j) A thin strip of leather   t.....

7. Combining Sentences

Join each of the pairs of sentences together using 'which' or 'that'.
    The blade was thick at the point.
    It had a sharp edge.

The blade, **which** was thick at the point, had a sharp edge.

(a) (i) I saw two more giant devilfish along the reef that summer.
    (ii) I did not try to spear them.
(b) (i) Even on land the devilfish can injure you.
    (ii) It is strong and does not dies quickly.
(c) (i) Rontu had rushed forward and seized the devilfish.
    (ii) The devilfish was too heavy to lift or shake.
(d) (i) The hand was free.
    (ii) The hand held the knife.
(e) (i) These arms can drag you under and hold you there until you drown.
    (ii) These arms have rows of suckers underneath them.
(f) (i) The head rose out of the twisting arms.
    (ii) The head was like a giant stalk.
(g) (i) I could hear the snapping of his beak.
    (ii) It was sharper than the knife I held in my hand.

The October Child
Eleanor Spence

THE CHILDREN'S BOOK COUNCIL OF AUSTRALIA
BOOK OF THE YEAR
1977

9. At the Playground

What happens when an autistic child is born into an average family? (An autistic child seems to live in a world of its own, out of touch with reality.) The arrival of baby, Carl, into the Mariner household produces just such a situation. 'The October Child' is an unsentimental yet sensitive story of the family's attempts to cope.

In this extract, Douglas is with his little brother Carl, at a children's playground.

The big rocker-swing nearby was still occupied by a group of boys and girls, working up one last effort of momentum. Heads were craned in mid-flight to watch Douglas's attempts at detaching Carl from the swing.

'Get *off*!' Douglas ordered, trying not to shout.

Accidentally or otherwise, Carl's foot caught his knee-cap, and he gasped at the sudden pain. He could hear giggles from the rocker-swing, and one boy called:

'Come on, mate! You ain't scared of a kid that size, are you?'

Heroically, Douglas ignored them all. Changing his tactics, he closed in on Carl from behind, and hauled him bodily off the swing, risking further damage from flailing feet. Once he was sure he had a firm grip, he made for the street.

So far, so good — but he could hardly carry Carl all the way home. At a safe distance from the playground, he cautiously let the child slide to the pavement, keeping a good hold on one arm. For one blessed moment, Carl stopped screaming; at the same time, he made a rapid about-turn, and tried to run back to the playground.

'We're going *home*, Carl! It's time for your bath!'

Carl was in no mood to listen, let alone understand. He pounded his feet on the pavement, and bellowed.

'No, Carl! We're *not* going back to the swing — we're going home!'

Carl swung round and clung with his free hand to the nearest railing. And Douglas realized the major cause of his wrath — the red ring was missing. It must have been dropped unnoticed near the swing.

Douglas hesitated for an instant. It was cold, and the sun was setting. He longed for the warmth and security of home. Moreover, he simply could not face the thought of going back to the playground to face anew the jeers of the children on the rocker-swing. He could still hear them in the distance, laughing and shouting.

'You've got lots more rings at home,' he told his brother. 'Now come *on*!'

Carl went berserk. He hooked his feet in the gaps between the railings and held grimly to the top of the fence with one hand, then began to batter his head with audible force against the iron, shrieking with the concentrated intensity of some caged wild animal.

They were in front of an old weatherboard house that had stood empty for months, but there were lights shining from the homes on either side. A woman put her head out of the front door and shouted at Douglas:

'Get that kid away from here before I call the police! He's just woken up my baby!'

In the other house, a dog began to growl threateningly — it sounded like a German Shepherd. Douglas shivered.

'Carl, please come!' he pleaded. 'Come home with me. Please, Carl!'

He held out his arms. Carl's hair flashed golden in the lamplight as his head swung round, and he fastened his teeth in his brother's wrist, ripping like tissue-paper the worn flannelette of Douglas's shirt.

Douglas stumbled backwards. He stared at the small upraised face of his brother, and could see in the round blue eyes nothing but rage and hate. There was no fear, no remorse — worst of all, there was no recognition. It was the face of a hostile stranger.

'You're *not* my brother!' Douglas whispered. 'You never *were* my brother!'

He turned and ran.

ELEANOR SPENCE, *The October Child*

At the Playground 65

1. Reading for Meaning

(a) Why did Douglas try to sound as if he was *not* shouting when he first spoke to Carl?
(b) How did Douglas feel as he tried to persuade Carl to come?
(c) What reason did Douglas give Carl for his having to go home?
(d) What was 'the major cause' of Carl's wrath?
(e) Give two reasons why Douglas decided not to return to the playground to look for Carl's ring.
(f) What caused Carl to go 'berserk'?
(g) What were *two* results of Carl's tantrum outside the old weatherboard house?
(h) Did Douglas run away from Carl because his younger brother had bitten him, or was there more to it? If so, what?
(i) Find at least *one* incident in this extract that shows Douglas was cautious. Explain how it shows this.
(j) Using this extract as a basis, try to list some of the features of an autistic child.

2. Word Forms

Use the appropriate form of the word in brackets to complete each of the sentences below.

(a) The driver made an .... effort to keep off the loose gravel. [intensity]
(b) Very few of the guests were .... personalities. [recognition]
(c) With the breakdown of the peace pact, ... were resumed between the two countries. [hostile]
(d) .... of the facts led most people to misjudge the man. [ignored]
(e) .... for mercy, the prisoner was taken away. [pleaded]
(f) A remarkable act of .... was responsible for saving the two fishermen. [heroically]
(g) The .... of the historical building was preferred to its destruction. [occupied]
(h) The fishermen on this occasion took a good .... of fish. [hauled]

3. Place in the Right Order

The following incidents all occur in the extract. However, they are in a jumbled order. Put them into the order in which they occur in the extract.

(a) A lady shouts at Douglas.
(b) Douglas realizes Carl's red ring is missing.
(c) Carl kicks Douglas's knee-cap.
(d) Douglas sees hatred in Carl's eyes.
(e) Heads turn to watch Douglas try to get Carl off the swing.
(f) Douglas lowers Carl to the ground.
(g) Carl bangs his head on the railings.
(h) A dog barks.
(i) Carl bites Douglas.
(j) Children tease Douglas.
(k) Carl stops screaming.
(l) Douglas carries Carl.

4. Character Description

Using the extract as a guide, separate the following box of words into these 3 columns.

DESCRIBES DOUGLAS	DESCRIBES CARL	DESCRIBES NEITHER
guilty	resentful,	annoying
helpful	rebellious	worried
responsible	sarcastic	cheerful
mature	aggressive	confident
protective	anxious	hostile
unreasonable	stubborn	dutiful

At the Playground 67

5. Word Families

Complete the word-family table below. The first one is done for you.

	NOUN	VERB	ADJECTIVE	ADVERB
	threat	threaten	threatening	threateningly
(a)		—		accidentally
(b)				cautiously
(c)	intensity			
(d)	remorse	—		
(e)		—	hostile	
(f)		hesitate		
(g)	security			
(h)	wrath	—		
(i)			empty	

6. Mystery Word

MYSTERY WORD: ....

(a) Use the letters already provided to help you fill in the blanks, using words from the box below.
(b) Take the letters in the shaded squares and re-arrange them to find the mystery boxed word.

occupied	hostile	swing
berserk	security	flailing
audible	recognition	anew
pleaded	momentum	threateningly
concentrated	detaching	warmth
intensity	accidentally	tactics
heroically	unnoticed	

At the Playground

7. Words and Their Meanings

Find words in the extract which have the same meaning as the following. The first letter of each word is given to help you. The first one is done for you.

	MEANING	EXTRACT WORD
(a)	Unfastening or removing	Detaching
(b)	Carefully; with attention to safety	C...............
(c)	Again; in a different way	A...............
(d)	Procedure designed to achieve something	T...............
(e)	The impetus gained by movement	M...............
(f)	Sorrow for a wrong committed	R...............
(g)	Wild; in a mad frenzy	B...............
(h)	Unfriendly; opposed	H...............
(i)	Brought together at one point	C...............
(j)	Footpath	P...............

8. Spelling Doubles

Each of the words below contains a double letter and is to be found in the extract. Use the letter clues given to help you find the words.

(a) _ cc _ _ _ _ _ _ (b) _ _ gg _ _ _ (c) _ cc _ _ _ _ _ _ ll _
(d) _ _ _ ss _ _ (e) _ _ ll _ _ _ _ (f) _ nn _ _ _ _ _ _
(g) _ ee _ _ (h) _ _ tt _ _ (i) _ _ _ nn _ _ _ tt _

Flambards
K. M. Peyton

10. Flying Machine

It is 1912 and the unexpected appearance of a flying machine over a country race meeting creates havoc for both horses and riders — especially when the pilot begins to lose control . . .

His arrival created immediate havoc. Christina was aware of it almost as soon as she set eyes on *Emma Four* by the nervous plunge beneath her of the calm Woodpigeon. She reined him in sharply, talked to him soothingly and stroked his neck, her eyes switching from William to the horses completing the race.

Firedance and Treasure had just cleared the big ditch which formed the last obstacle, and were starting neck and neck up the long run-in. The crowd's roar had changed to a frantic, amazed gabble. Christina watched, her eyes widening with a dreadful anticipation, as the harmless afternoon's entertainment suddenly took on an almost comic inevitability. So intimately concerned with the chief participants, she nevertheless felt completely detached, utterly unable to do anything to help either Mark or William at these separate crises of their lives.

The crowd started to run. They ran in all directions, some aimlessly, still watching the stricken *Emma Four*, pointing and gesticulating, some in real, screaming panic. The aeroplane came down over the valley, very low, her wings rolling horribly, engine screaming. All the horses tied to the farm-carts started to plunge and whinny madly, some breaking away. Christina saw one gallop full tilt into the tea tent by one opening, and out with a frightful crashing noise in its wake through the other. One horse, still between the shafts of a smart gig, bolted down the hill and got stuck in the stream. Firedance and Treasure, one moment galloping towards this monstrous, screaming apparition, were now bolting headlong back down the valley. Firedance ran himself to a standstill, and Peter was able to fling himself off and hold his head, but Treasure, mad with fright, would not stop for the hedge and stream at the bottom and went straight through the obstacle as if it did not exist. Mark was flung violently from the saddle by a blow from a low branch, and fell heavily down the bank below, leaving ribbons of yellow silk speared on the thorn hedge like breaking willow buds.

Christina watched the whole sequence from Woodpigeon's back with a sense of doom, utterly calm because there was nothing she could do. She winced for Mark, and turned to watch William make his forced landing, so close to her now that she could see the tense look on his face, the stiff leg[1] stuck out in its awkward fashion in front of him.

She could tell that he had picked the flat spot at the finish to put *Emma Four* down on, but at the angle he was coming to it, it was very short, for a hedge ran beyond it, dividing the grazing on the hill itself. Worse than that, a group of panic-stricken women chose at the last moment to run in the wrong direction. Christina bit her lip, drawing blood, as *Emma Four* roared towards them. Their skirts flew up, revealing white petticoats and long, stalky legs like the legs of panicking hens that she had seen running before the de Dion.[2] Christina clenched her hands on the reins and cried out, 'William!'

Emma Four's engine roared. William was too low to turn, and had no alternative but to put the aeroplane's nose up and clear the women by flying over them. They had the sense to throw themselves down on the ground (or they fainted with fright, Christina was never sure which) and *Emma Four's* skids went over them with about five feet to spare. It was as if she threw her nose up as a last dying gesture to please, for immediately the engine cut out again and she nosedived into the thorn hedge beyond. Her tail cartwheeled, one wing dug in with a sickening rending of cracking timber. Burying her nose deep into the hedge, *Emma Four* then rolled over, and came to rest upside-down, her undercarriage wheels spinning against the sky.

The scattered crowd now, with a whoop, started to run back in *Emma Four's* direction, babbling and shouting with excitement. But Christina, spurring Woodpigeon with such urgency that he did not think to hesitate, arrived by the stricken aircraft first. She flung herself off the horse and peered into the hedge.

'William!'

William's face, ludicrously surprised, was staring back at her, upside-down. He was still in his seat, suspended by his webbing lap-strap.

'Are you all right?'

'Yes, thank you,' he said very politely.

K. M. PEYTON, *Flambards*

---

[1] As a young boy, William smashed his knee in a hunting accident.
[2] An early model motor car.

Flying Machine 73

1. Reading for Meaning

(a) Who or what is 'Emma Four'?

(b) Christina is 'unable to do anything to help either Mark or William at these separate crises of their lives'. Explain the crises that arrive for both these young men.

(c) When the crowd started to run in all directions, some people acted in one way; some in another. What are the two different ways they acted?

(d) Three things are noted about the aeroplane as it comes down over the valley. What are they?

(e) Describe, in your own words, how two of the farm-cart horses got into trouble.

(f) Why does Christina remain 'utterly calm' as she watches what happens to Mark?

(g) What unexpected happening causes William to put up the aeroplane's nose at the last moment?

(h) Is Christina right or wrong in going to help William rather than Mark? Give a reason for the answer you choose.

(i) Choose a word from the passage that describes the mood (feeling) of the crowd *after* the plane has come down.

(j) What is unexpected about William's reply to Christina?

2. Dictionary Work

Match up the words from the column on the left with their meanings on the right. Often only the essential word or words have been taken from the fuller item in your back-of-the-book dictionary. So, use the dictionary to help you match up to the job!

	WORD	MEANING
(a)	anticipation	unconnected
(b)	entertainment	waving the hands around
(c)	inevitability	a one-horse carriage
(d)	intimately	expectation
(e)	participants	without purpose
(f)	detached	a series of happenings
(g)	utterly	personally
(h)	separate	choice
(i)	crises	ripping
(j)	aimlessly	amusement
(k)	gesticulating	comically
(l)	gig	flinched
(m)	apparition	clumsy
(n)	sequence	completely
(o)	winced	moments of extreme danger
(p)	awkward	the certainty of a happening
(q)	alternative	great need
(r)	rending	those who take part in
(s)	urgency	a weird appearance
(t)	ludicrously	apart

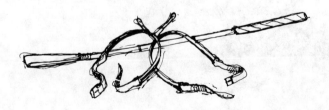

3. Context

Show that you understand the meanings of the words in Exercise 2 by filling in the blank spaces.

(a) Christina watched with a dreadful ....
(b) She felt completely .... from the events she was forced to watch.
(c) People were pointing and ....
(d) William's face looked .... surprised.
(e) Christina watched .... calm because there was nothing she could do.
(f) This monstrous, screaming ....
(g) One horse was between the shafts of a smart ....
(h) One wing dug in with a sickening .... of cracking timber.
(i) William was too low to turn and had no .... but to put the aeroplane's nose up.
(j) She .... for Mark as she saw him fall.
(k) Christina spurred on her horse with great ....
(l) The stiff leg stuck out in its .... fashion in front of him.
(m) The harmless afternoon's .... suddenly took on an almost comic ....
(n) Neither Mark nor William could be helped at these .... crises of their lives.
(o) Some of the crowd ran ....
(p) She was .... concerned with the chief .... in the afternoon's events.
(q) Neither Mark nor William could be helped at these separate .... of their lives.
(r) From Treasure's bolting to Mark's fall — she watched the whole .... from her horse.

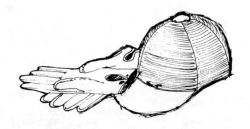

4. Spelling

Now that you've dealt with the meanings of the twenty words in Ex. 2, try doing a little spelling work with them

(a) Find the six words from Ex. 2 that **share an 'i'**:

(b) **Care for a Clue?**
   (i) that has a 'pain'.
   (ii) that is spelt the same backwards as forwards.
   (iii) that includes a four-letter friend.
   (iv) that ends in a big hospital room.
   (v) that begins with a word meaning 'against' and also includes a word meaning 'a light touch with the hand'.

(c) **Equals**

Find words from Ex. 2 by solving the equations and unjumbling.
   (i) $2(p+i+a+t)+rc+ns = \ldots$
   (ii) $2(g+t+i)+cu+lanes = \ldots$
   (iii) $2(a+p+i)+t+ron = \ldots$
   (iv) $2(a+e+t)+rl+vin = \ldots$

5. Adjectives ⇄ Nouns

The nouns below have adjectives that go with them in the passage. Link up each adjective and noun.

	ADJECTIVE	NOUN
(a)	chief	wheels
(b)	low	hedge
(c)	willow	spot
(d)	thorn	branch
(e)	calm	tent
(f)	comic	buds
(g)	flat	direction
(h)	tea	inevitability
(i)	wrong	participants
(j)	undercarriage	Woodpigeon

These same adjectives can easily become nouns, given the right (sentence) conditions. Write down the following sentences inserting, in the blanks, the adjectives-turned-nouns from the left-hand column above.

(k) The .... by the river was an ideal place for the tents.
(l) The wind dropped but it was only the .... before the storm.
(m) The .... wore head feathers and face paint.
(n) The weather bureau announced that the high would be followed by a ....
(o) The .... is known as 'the tree that weeps'.
(p) The police argued that the motorist was obviously in the ....
(q) No rose without a ....
(r) .... will be served with scones and cream.
(s) The plane's .... was out of order and could not be lifted.
(t) Read a .... in class and you'll be in trouble.

Word Skills One

6. Straight Down the Middle

Below is a list of events from the passage. In your workbook, rearrange the events so that they are actually in the order in which they happen in the passage.

(a) The crowd starts to run back towards the plane.
(b) Mark is flung from the saddle.
(c) The women fling themselves on the ground.
(d) Woodpigeon plunges nervously.
(e) The plane comes to rest upside-down.
(f) The farm-cart horses go mad.
(g) The crowd starts to run.
(h) The women panic and run in the wrong direction.
(i) The crowd's roar changes to a gabble.
(j) William thanks her politely.
(k) The plane passes over the women with very little room to spare.
(l) The plane comes down very low over the valley.
(m) Christina peers into the hedge.
(n) Christina turns to watch William make his landing.
(o) Firedance and Treasure bolt down the valley.
(p) Christina watches Mark from Woodpigeon's back.
(q) Christina is first to arrive at the plane.

7. Mixed-Up Lines

The lines below have been mixed up, but, properly linked, they will give you a summary of the story in *Flambards*. See if you can join the lines correctly in your workbook. To help you a little, the first and last words of the summary are in italics.

(a) Flambards.
(b) before the First World War:
(c) *Twelve*-year-old orphan Christina
(d) It is a strange, unruly household
(e) and be totally bound up *with*.
(f) is sent to live with her Uncle Russell

(g) one she comes to love, hate
(h) that Christina grows up in
(i) and his two sons in their old country house,
(j) during those years

8. It's a Noisy Passage!

Well, what else would you expect from a passage with both a horse race and a plane crash?

As you read through the passage, you'll notice that the writer has used a variety of words dealing with noises. This kind of variety in vocabulary is essential if a piece of writing is to stay fresh and interesting.

Draw up the long boxes in your workbook. Then, using the clues, supply the noisy words from top to bottom.

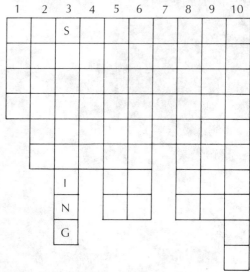

Clues: 1 is a kind of shout which changes to 2 and shares a letter with it.
In 3 you are given the first letter and the last three letters.
4 is a sound that goes with plunging horses.
5 is the sound of crockery breaking.
The sound of timber breaking is word 6.
The crowd runs with a ... back to the plane (7).
8 and 9 are both 'ing' words denoting things done with excitement by the crowd.
10 is the tone of voice in which Christina spoke to Woodpigeon when the plane first came into view.

The Nargun and the Stars

PATRICIA WRIGHTSON

SIMON

11. The Nargun

In Wongadilla, Simon Brent came to know the spirits of the swamps and the mountains. Here, too, he first encountered the Nargun . . . and its frightening power.

Behind the noise of the tractor he felt again that stillness of the night when he had met the Nargun: that second when his mind and skin and blood all listened to the waiting silence.

They swung back east — and that was surely a flash of light from the end of the mountain? Charlie's torch? Simon banged Edie's shoulder and pointed. She nodded hard — she had seen it too. But now they were passing the gully, which they should have been watching instead of Charlie's torch. Simon screwed up his eyes again; Edie slowed to a crawl while she craned anxiously; the tractor stalled. Silence closed on them like a trap.

'Curse!' muttered Edie, fumbling with the controls; and Simon whispered, 'Shush! Not yet!' He stilled the singing of his ears to listen. There was something deep and strong, too low to hear: a *whmp, whmp, whmp* that was not his heart. Was that what he had felt in the silence? Could it be the Nargun? He knew at once that it was not. Nothing about the Nargun had that machine-like regularity; it might be the bulldozer, perhaps. But what was that other sound that he could not hear? What else was there?

All his life and being reached out listening to the night. No feather floating down from any tree; no cricket moving under any stone. Was it the mountain stirring? . . . darkness flowing? What moved?

In one more heart-beat he knew. Edie had managed to start the motor *bang . . . bang . . . bang*. Simon shrieked, '*Edie! Jump!*' And the cry of the Nargun sprang at them from the gully.

Nga-a-a!

Simon leapt from the tractor and dragged at Edie who was tumbling out. They dragged and pushed each other behind a tree while the great dark shape thudded at the tractor. Stumpy limbs crashed at metal, the motor spat and roared and died; headlights swung as the tractor toppled over. Rock fists smashed at it, and the Nargun raised its snout and bellowed at the stars.

Terror turned Simon's hands to steel, grasping at Edie and dragging her through the dark to a farther tree. They saw Charlie's torch wobbling fast across the mountain and that was another terror — he would go stumbling straight into the monster! Simon dragged out his own torch and flashed it once; that was all he could do in case it brought the ancient monster thundering after himself and Edie. He crushed her against the tree, and her own hands were steel holding him there too. They breathed jerkily.

Charlie's torch had vanished. There was darkness except for the overturned headlights; and then a tearing and leaping of flame that lit the gully mouth and made the trees jump. The tractor was burning, and the Nargun lurched erect in the flames and bellowed with pride.

PATRICIA WRIGHTSON, The Nargun and the Stars

1. Reading for Meaning

(a) 'They swung back east ....' Simon and Edie were, at this point,
    (i) walking.
    (ii) driving a car.
    (iii) riding on a tractor.
    (iv) driving a bulldozer.

(b) They should have been watching the gully because
    (i) they knew the Nargun would come from there.
    (ii) there were pot-holes near the gully.
    (iii) there was a bulldozer coming down it.
    (iv) it was particularly dark in the gully.

(c) Which one of the following did *not* distract them when they should have been watching the gully?
    (i) Charlie's torch
    (ii) The stalling of the tractor
    (iii) The crickets
    (iv) The sound of the bulldozer motor

(d) 'In one more heartbeat he knew.' This means Simon
    (i) knew the cause of the bulldozer sound.
    (ii) could sense the Nargun was there about to attack.
    (iii) knew the tractor would not start properly.
    (iv) understood why the mountain was stirring.

(e) Simon and Edie hid behind a tree because
  (i) the Nargun would not destroy trees.
  (ii) they were terrified and it was the nearest place where they could hide.
  (iii) they wanted to see what the Nargun would do.
  (iv) it was huge and the Nargun would not be able to smash it.
(f) The 'ancient monster' in this story is
  (i) the old tractor.
  (ii) the Nargun.
  (iii) Charlie.
  (iv) the mountain on which the events took place.
(g) Simon grabbed Edie and led her to safety because he
  (i) was a calm, cool thinker even in the midst of danger.
  (ii) did not want her to see the full fury of the Nargun.
  (iii) did not want Charlie to think he was irresponsible.
  (iv) was terrified and this forced him to act to make them both safe.
(h) At the first sighting of Charlie's torch Simon was
  (i) thankful, because it meant Charlie was alive.
  (ii) relieved, because Charlie would be able to see where he was going.
  (iii) terrified, because he thought Charlie might blunder into the Nargun.
  (iv) anxious, because Charlie might be seen by the monster.
(i) 'Rock fists smashed at it' . . . If this is *literally* true it means that
  (i) the Nargun is made of rock.
  (ii) the Nargun is made of something hard, like rock.
  (iii) the Nargun's fists are able to smash rock.
  (iv) the Nargun's fists could rock the tractor.
(j) 'The tractor was burning. . .' This was most likely caused by
  (i) the petrol tank igniting from sparks created as the Nargun smashed away at the tractor.
  (ii) the Nargun deliberately setting fire to the tractor.
  (iii) the battery terminals shorting across to the magneto.
  (iv) a cigarette butt left by them in the tractor.

2. Put the Sentences Back Together

Select one correct phrase or clause from each of the columns overleaf, put them together and so re-form sentences from the passage.

84 Word Skills One

(a)	Rock fists smashed at it	grasping at Edie and dragging her through the dark	who was tumbling out.
(b)	They swung back east —	and her own hands were steel	and bellowed in pride.
(c)	Terror turned Simon's hands to steel,	and the Nargun raised its snout	holding him there too.
(d)	Simon leapt from the tractor	and the Nargun lurched erect in the flames	at the tractor.
(e)	They dragged and pushed each other behind a tree	and that surely was a flash of light	and bellowed at the stars.
(f)	The tractor was burning,	while the great, dark shape thudded	to a farther tree.
(g)	He crushed her against the tree,	and dragged at Edie	from the end of the mountain?

3. Word-Sort

Sort the words below into their correct places in the grid. Most of the words come from the story or are suggested by it. Each word chosen must begin with the letter at the top of the column.

uncertain	grabbed	night
against	ancient	rock
regular	near	nodded
Nargun	gully	uproar
anger	noisy	nervous
arched	raised	under
understood	great	noticed

	N	A	R	G	U	N
NOUN (naming word)	night					
VERB (action word)						
ADJECTIVE (describing word)						
PREPOSITION						

4. Power-Packed Verbs!

Take each one of the following power-packed verbs from the passage and match it with the correct clue from the boxed column below.

```
thudded      shrieked
lurched      toppled
crashed      spat
crushed      bellowed
```

	CLUE	VERB
(a)	The great dark shape .... at the tractor.	Thudded
(b)	With pride the Nargun gave its cry.	....
(c)	The Nargun's stumpy limbs .... at the tractor's metal.	....
(d)	How the tractor fell over.	....
(e)	Thus Simon held Edie against the tree.	....
(f)	The Nargun .... erect in the flames.	....
(g)	The way the tractor motor sounded as the Nargun attacked.	....
(h)	Simon screamed this way at Edie.	....

5. Tricky Twins

The words 'stalled' and 'stilled' are both used in the extract. Here they are, used in their correct sentences.

   The tractor **stalled**.

   He **stilled** the singing of his ears.

Below are some more 'tricky twins', each pair having two sentences with them. Write out each sentence, and fit the correct one from each pair into the blank space.

(a) **singing/singeing**
- (i) You could see the fire .... the paintwork.
- (ii) They hear the birds .... in the trees.

(b) **soldier/solder**
- (i) The .... was used to join the wires together.
- (ii) There was a row of medals on the chest of the ....

(c) **tied/tired**
- (i) The heroine was .... to the railway tracks.
- (ii) Simon's whole body was .... from the unusual exertion.

(d) **whether/weather**
- (i) They were uncertain .... they would ever see the Nargun again or not.
- (ii) Charlie cast a quick eye up at the ....

(e) **taught/taut**
- (i) The fence-wire was .... with the strain.
- (ii) It was the first lesson he had been .... by the monster.

(f) **sole/soul**
- (i) Their .... purpose was to get the Nargun to move elsewhere.
- (ii) It seemed the creature had a .... of iron.

(g) **siege/seize** (watch the spelling!)
- (i) They prepared for a long wait as they laid .... to the cave.
- (ii) They saw Simon leap and .... his torch before turning in terror.

(h) **storey/story**
- (i) The .... proved to be an absorbing one.
- (ii) The fourth .... of the building was gutted by fire.

6. Punctuation

Correctly punctuate the following passage.

its in there whispered simon whatll happen not what we planned anyhow said Charlie and im not going in to find out bad enough with a torch and no nargun they waited and listened now one and now another putting an ear to the rock.

7. Changing the Tenses

The extract is written with its verbs in the *past tense* — as though the events being described happened in the past. If it were written as though it were actually happening in the present, the *present tense* of each verb would have to be used. Change each of the following sentences or clauses from the past to the present tense. The first one is done for you. The verbs you need to change are in bold type.

Past Tense: He **felt** again that stillness of the night.
Present Tense: He **feels** again that stillness of the night.

(a) They **swung** back east.
(b) She **had seen** it too.
(c) Simon **screwed** up his eyes again.
(d) He **knew** at once that it was not.
(e) Simon **shrieked** 'Edie! Jump!'
(f) The cry of the Nargun **sprang** at them.
(g) Simon **leapt** from the tractor.
(h) . . . then a tearing and leaping of flame that **lit** the gully mouth.
(i) The motor **spat** and **roared** and **died**.

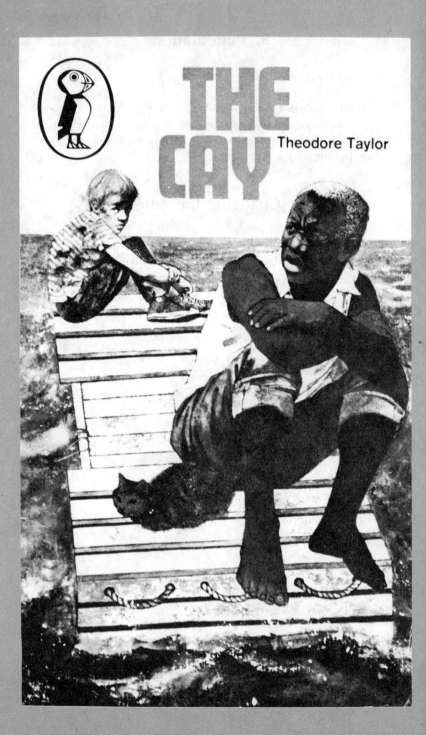

12. Torpedoed

'The Cay' describes the adventures of Phillip, a young white boy adrift on a raft on the ocean and marooned on the Cay with Timothy, an old Negro seaman. This passage describes the sinking of Phillip's ship.

We were torpedoed at about three o'clock in the morning on 6 April 1942, two days after leaving Panama.

I was thrown from the top bunk and suddenly found myself on my hands and knees on the deck. We could hear the ship's whistle blowing constantly, and there were sounds of metal wrenching and much shouting. The whole ship was shuddering. It felt as though we'd stopped and were dead in the water.

My mother was very calm, not at all like she was at home. She talked quietly while she got dressed, telling me to tie my shoes, and be certain to carry my wool sweater, and to put on my leather jacket. Her hands were not shaking.

She helped me put on my life jacket, then put hers on, saying, 'Now, remember everything that we were told about abandoning ship.' The officers had held drills every day.

As she was speaking, there was another violent explosion. We were thrown against the cabin door, which the steward had warned us not to lock because it might become jammed. We pushed it open and went out to the boat deck, which was already beginning to tilt.

Everything was bright red, and there were great crackling noises. The entire afterpart of the ship was on fire, and sailors were launching the lifeboat that was on our deck. Steam lines had broken, and the steam was hissing out. Heat from the fire washed over us.

When the lifeboat had been swung out, the captain came down from the bridge. He was a small, wiry white-haired man and was acting the way I'd been told captains should act. He stood by the lifeboat in the fire's glow, very alert, giving orders to the crew. He was carrying a briefcase and a navigation instrument I knew to be a sextant. On the other side of the ship, another lifeboat was being launched.

Near us, two sailors with axes chopped, at lines, and two big life rafts plunged towards the water, which looked black except for pools of fire from burning fuel oil.

The captain shouted, 'Get a move on! Passengers into the boats!' Tins of lubricating oil in the afterholds had ignited and were exploding, but the ones forward had not been exposed to the fire.

A sailor grabbed my mother's hand and helped her in, and then I felt myself being passed into the hands of a sailor on the boat. The other passengers were helped in, and someone yelled, 'Lower away'. At that moment, the *Hato* lurched heavily and something happened to the boat falls.

The bow tilted downwards, and the next thing I knew we were all in the water. I saw my mother near me and yelled to her. Then something hit me from above.

A long time later (four hours I was told), I opened my eyes to see blue sky above. It moved back and forth, and I could hear the slap of water. I had a terrible pain in my head. I closed my eyes again, thinking maybe I was dreaming. Then a voice said, 'Young bahss, how are you feelin'?'

I turned my head.

I saw a huge, very old Negro sitting on the raft near me.

THEODORE TAYLOR, *The Cay*

1. Reading for Meaning

(a) What happened to Phillip when the ship was torpedoed?
(b) What sounds suggested that the ship could be sinking?
(c) How did Phillip's mother react when the ship was torpedoed?
(d) How do you know that the passengers had been prepared for the emergency of the ship's sinking?
(e) Why had the steward warned them not to lock the cabin door?
(f) How does the captain react to the torpedoing of his ship?
(g) Why was it likely that the ship would explode?
(h) How did Phillip come to finish up in the water?
(i) Why did Phillip have a terrible pain in his head?
(j) What is the meaning of these words?
    (i) tilt   (ii) constantly
    (iii) wrenching   (iv) exposed
    (You may like to consult the dictionary in the back of the book.)

2. Nouns

Write down the nouns that come from these words. The first one has been done to help you.

(a)	quietly [quietness]	(i)	dressed
(b)	suddenly	(j)	certain
(c)	hear	(k)	helped
(d)	thrown	(l)	bright
(e)	warned	(m)	washed
(f)	remember	(n)	alert
(g)	told	(o)	heavily
(h)	felt	(p)	tilted

3. Jumbled Events

The events of the story are out of order. See whether you can rearrange them in their correct order.

(a) Phillip was hit on the head.
(b) Phillip was thrown from the top bunk.
(c) The passengers in the lifeboat were spilled into the water.
(d) The captain came down from the bridge.
(e) Phillip saw an old Negro sailor sitting on the raft near him.
(f) Phillip and his mother put on their life jackets.
(g) A sailor helped Phillip's mother into a lifeboat. Phillip and his mother went out onto the boat deck.

4. Subjects

Match the **subjects** in the left-hand column with their correct endings (**predicates**) in the right-hand column to form sentences based on the story.

	SUBJECT	PREDICATE
(a)	My mother	came down from the bridge.
(b)	The officers	grabbed my mother's hand.
(c)	The captain	hit me from above.
(d)	A sailor	had ignited.
(e)	The *Hato*	had warned us not to lock the cabin door.
(f)	Another lifeboat	had held drills every day.
(g)	Something	was very calm.
(h)	Tins of lubricating oil	lurched heavily.
(i)	The steam	was being launched.
(j)	The steward	was hissing out.

5. Pronouns

In the box are pronouns. Using the information of the story, write down the sentences and insert the correct pronouns from the box in the blank spaces. You can only use each pronoun once.

PRONOUNS			
I	me	my	myself
he	she	it	they our

(a) I saw my mother near ....
(b) .... were exploding.
(c) .... was a small, wiry white-haired man.
(d) .... had a terrible pain in my hand.
(e) Sailors were launching the lifeboat that was on .... deck.

Torpedoed 93

(f) I found .... on .... hands and knees on the deck.
(g) .... might become jammed.
(h) My mother was very calm, not at all like .... was at home.

6. Spelling

Write down these spelling words and then do the following exercise based on these words.

abandoning	navigation
already	exposed
quietly	beginning

(a) This word contains a man's name.
(b) The middle of this word is what models do.
(c) This word rhymes with steady.
(d) The middle of this word has an alcoholic drink.
(e) This word is connected with sailing ships or flying planes.
(f) This word is the opposite of noisily.

7. Completing the Sentences

Complete these sentences, using your knowledge of the story. Notice that each part to be completed is an incomplete adjectival clause beginning with 'who', 'whose', 'which', or 'that'.

(a) Passengers could hear the ship's whistle, which ....
(b) We were thrown against the cabin door, which ....
(c) The captain who .... gave orders to the crew.
(d) Tins of lubricating oil, that ...., had exploded.
(e) A very old negro, who ...., said, 'Young bahss, how are you feeling'?'
(f) Steam was hissing out of the lines that ....
(g) In the water Phillip yelled to his mother, who ....
(h) Heat, which .... washed over us.

13. Bushfire

The day is unbearably hot and dead calm: a day when there is a total fire ban. Only one spark will start a wild, devouring fire that would destroy everything in its path: homes, livestock, people . . .

The raging, uncontrollable wildfire sweeps across dry grassland and dense eucalypt forest, and the Mob — Pete, Bill, Jan, Steve and Fizzer — find themselves fighting together for their lives.

They plunged on. Sometimes they were engulfed in clouds of smoke like stinking yellow mountain mist, but Bill knew the way so well that he went forward unerringly.

Suddenly he stopped. 'Listen! A coo-ee!'

The long-drawn-out first syllable floated to them on the smoke, followed by the whip-like ending.

'Jan?'

Jan was coo-eeing. It did not sound very loud; there were too many other noises to drown the call.

They listened. Each coo-ee came nearer. It was unlikely that she thought they would be on this track; probably she wanted anyone at all who might be in this vicinity to know she was there.

'She's coming back — coming this way!'

Then Jan came out of the smoke. She was crying, and so distraught that she didn't ask how or why they were there. Perhaps she understood. Shane was their friend, too.

'Fire's right across the track! We can't get through!'

'How near?'

'Quarter of a mile, p'raps. Not burning as fast now. But creeping up over everything, swallowing everything. I saw a koala burn . . .' She stopped briefly, then went on talking fast. 'Like you did, Bill. It just kept going up and up the tree . . . alight. A very tall tree . . . and the crown was burning. Until I couldn't see it any more. And it was crying all the way, like a baby.'

They both sensed the quiver of her body. And Bill went back in thought ten years.

'I can't get through. I can't get through to Shane!' Jan was streaked with grime and smoke and tears. Along the route she had lost her scarf, but she was still carrying the axe Bill had seen in her hand, and which had told him where she was heading.

Now they realized that the wind was not altogether subdued by the cold front. That a fierce gust had arisen again, and fire was spotting over their heads. Fire-brands were lobbing behind them. A series of missiles, as though the fire had suddenly found its mark, and was aiming with accuracy. It would veer again but not before its mischief had been done. It had all the viciousness of fire out of control . . . of wildfire.

Bill knew, and the others were scarcely less quick to realize, that retreat was cut off.

MAVIS THORPE CLARK, *Wildfire*

1. Reading for Meaning

(a) Bill knew the way along the track so well that
 (i) he was able to keep them all running.
 (ii) he only had to stop occasionally to check his bearings.
 (iii) he made no mistakes in leading the others.
 (iv) the others felt quite safe with him.

(b) The call 'Coo-ee' was shouted with the first syllable
 (i) loud, and the second syllable soft.
 (ii) soft, and the second syllable loud.
 (iii) short and sharp, and the second syllable long.
 (iv) long, and the second syllable short and sharp.

(c) Jan's call did not sound very loud because
 (i) there was so much other noise around.
 (ii) she was out of breath.
 (iii) she was feeling weakened after her run.
 (iv) the smoke had affected everyone's hearing.

(d) Jan met the others on this bush track because
   (i) they had been trying to reach their friend, Shane.
   (ii) they were trying to escape a bushfire.
   (iii) there were no other tracks through the bush.
   (iv) they had arranged to meet.

(e) 'I saw a koala burn . . .' Jan stopped speaking briefly, after saying this because
   (i) she was still trying to recover her breath.
   (ii) she wondered if the others wanted to ask her about it.
   (iii) she knew the others would be upset at the thought.
   (iv) the memory of it still gave her the shudders.

(f) 'Bill went back in thought ten years'
   (i) to see if he could work out a solution to their predicament.
   (ii) and remembered an incident when he had seen a koala burn in a bushfire.
   (iii) because he suddenly felt very young and inexperienced.
   (iv) and felt ashamed of having cried then.

(g) Bill knew where Jan had been heading
   (i) because they had talked about it earlier.
   (ii) by the fact that she had lost her scarf.
   (iii) by the axe that she was carrying.
   (iv) because the path led to only one place.

(h) The cold front
   (i) had completely checked the fire.
   (ii) was due soon, so that the danger from the fire was actually diminishing.
   (iii) had only partially checked the fire.
   (iv) had not brought any rain.

(i) 'Fire was spotting over their heads' means
   (i) they could see spots of fire ahead.
   (ii) the fire was reduced to small areas.
   (iii) bits of burning tree were being blown over their heads.
   (iv) they could see spots of fire in the tall trees overhead.

(j) Bill was the first to realize that
   (i) they would have to hurry as the wind had freshened.
   (ii) the danger from the fire was increasing.
   (iii) they would not be able to outrun this fire.
   (iv) they could not go back the way they had come because of the bushfire.

2. 'Wildfire' Words

Below is a 'wildfire' passage. However, blanks have been left where the verbs should be, and an appropriate verb has been placed in brackets. You are to use the correct form of the given verb and so complete the passage.

'Partially .... [to ring] by fires the weary fox padded on, running from the wind. The fire behind him continued .... [to leap] from bush to bush, ... [to consume] everything in its path. He could feel its heat and hear it as it .... [to crackle] and .... [to roar], hungrily .... [to devour] even the forest giants. His tail had been .... [to singe] where a .... [to blaze] ember had landed, and his skin was .... [to shrivel] from the intense heat. Onward he pushed himself with a last weary effort, determined to avoid being .... [to encircle] by this scourge of the bush.'

3. Reporting Mix-Up!

Ace-reporter Henry Pootles, from the *Mullengudgery Meanderer*, has done it again! After interviewing Bill and the others to get details of what happened he has filed his report for his paper. But what a mix-up! Henry has so many details wrong, he may have set a new record! Your job is to rewrite his report, correcting any inaccuracies.

Mullengudgery Meanderer 15 August 1979

Amidst swirling green mist, John led his friends forward. A shout of 'help!' brought them to a halt and they were soon joined by their brother, Jane. Jane was laughing happily and asked the others why they were there. She reported that the fire was still half a mile away and burning faster than ever. She also reported that she'd seen a kangaroo burning. She was carrying a chain-saw. In the midst of this tense situation, John and the others suddenly became aware that the fire was going out. They would be able to return fairly easily.

4. Word Meanings

Each of the following words from the passage is surrounded by four possible meanings. Identify the correct meaning for each word and use it in a sentence to show your mastery of the word.

(a) **engulfed**: swallowed up / intensified, heightened / caused to blaze up / commanded

(b) **vicinity**: watchfulness / change of circumstances / South American mammal related to llama / surrounding area

(c) **unerringly**: without changing direction at all / confidently / without any mistakes / slowly and painstakingly

(d) **distraught**: violently agitated / mildly upset / lacking confidence / easily distracted

(e) **grime**: breaking the law / dirt, ingrained in some surface / thickness / small particles, or powder

(f) **subdued**: changed from solid to gas / conquered, overcome / surrendered / supplied missing words

(g) **lobbing**: regarding with disgust / entering the porch of a house / establishing in a place / pitching high into the air

5. Fire-Word Sort

Sort the words below into their correct places in the grid. Most of the words come from the extract, or are suggested by it. Each word chosen must begin with the letter at the top of the column, and each word must be used only once.

undergrowth	firebrands	swallowing
hasten	engulfed	use
insects	unkempt	indistinct
birds	rapid	embers
effective	hand	route
huge	scarf	injected
found	burn	fast
black	regained	slow

	B	U	S	H	F	I	R	E
DESCRIPTION WORD	black							
OBJECT								
ACTION WORD								

6. Plurals

When Jan meets the others, she has lost her scarf. 'Scarf' is one word that has two different forms for the plural — 'scarfs' or 'scarves'.

Most words ending in 'f' form their plural by changing the 'f' to 'v' and adding 'es'. However, watch out for the few exceptions! Form plurals for the following words.

(a) shelf (f) leaf (k) thief (p) knife
(b) calf (g) hoof (l) beef (q) wife
(c) handkerchief (h) wolf (m) loaf (r) elf
(d) half (i) life (n) oaf (s) sheaf
(e) wharf (j) reef (o) self (t) chief

7. Change the Form

Complete the following sentences by filling in the blanks, using an appropriate form of the word in brackets at the end of each sentence. The first one is done for you.

(a) He wiped his *grimy* hands on his sweat-soaked shirt. [grime]
(b) Slowly the .... dawned on him — they were trapped! [realize]
(c) The .... wind, playing a game with them, fanned the flames then died away. [mischief]
(d) The .... of water was proving to be their greatest problem. [scarcely]
(e) The wind .... to the north-west. [veer]
(f) As they stood, horror-stricken, flames began to .... the trees ahead. [engulfed]
(g) .... with fear, she turned to face the fierce heat. [quiver]
(h) Dazed and uncertain, they at last began to wonder how .... their directions had been. [accuracy]

The Goalkeeper's Revenge
and Other Stories

BILL NAUGHTON

14. Eating the Evidence

The boy who is telling this story works on the wharves. He has just been caught stealing oranges by a policeman nicknamed Pongo.

I got caught because the string of my brat* broke, and Pongo, after looking over my load, noticed my somewhat bulging pockets. He made me draw the pony-and-cart to one side, and then he took me in his cabin and went through my pockets. There were seventeen oranges in all, and he placed them carefully on the table.

'An example has to be made,' he said, 'of somebody or other — and I reckon you're the unlucky one. Now, my lad, what have you to say for yourself?'

I said nothing. I was dead frightened, but I forced myself to keep my mouth shut. I had read too many detective stories to make the mistake of blabbing. *Anything you say may be used in evidence against you.* I kept that firm in my mind, and I refused to be interrogated. Pongo, who did not care for my attitude, said, 'Righto, I'll go off and bring a colleague as a witness.' And with that he went, carefully locking the door behind him.

I felt awful then. It was the suspense. I looked at the walls, I looked at the door, and I looked at the seventeen oranges, and I looked at my brat with the broken string. I thought of how I would get sacked and get sentenced, and of what my mother would say and my father do.

There was no escape. I was there — and the evidence was there before me on the table — and Pongo had gone for his mate to be witness. I was ruined for life.

'Oh, my God,' I moaned in anguish, 'whatever shall I do?'

'*Eat 'em!*' spoke a voice in my head.

'Eh?' I asked. 'Eat 'em?'

'Yeh, that's right,' replied this inner voice — '*and then the evidence will be gone. But be quick about it.*'

I thought for half a second — then — snatched an orange, peeled it in a jiff, popped it in my mouth, crushed the juice out and swallowed it, swallowing the orange, and I was just about to squirt out the pips when the voice cried:

'*No!*'

'Eh?'

---

*Apron.

'*You have to swallow them too!*'

'What — the pips?'

'*Yes — peel an' all! evidence.*'

'Oh — oh, of course,' and I forced the pips to the back of my mouth and took a handful of peel to help get them down my gullet.

'*Don't bother to chew,*' said the voice, '*it's a race against time.*'

It certainly was. After that first orange I took out my penknife and slashed the fruit into chunks and gulped them down as fast as I could pick them up.

I was all but full to the brim, with three oranges still to go, when I heard Pongo and his mate coming back. With a sigh I gave up, but the voice warned me to guzzle on, suggesting that the more I ate the less evidence there would be — and as luck would have it, Pongo and his mate were detained over checking-up on some outgoing wagons, and since the sigh seemed to have cleared up a sort of traffic-jam in my oesophagus, I set about finishing off those last few, and by the time the key turned in the lock I was consuming the final piece of the seventeen oranges.

'This is him,' began Pongo to his mate, 'I caught him with his pockets ramjam full of oranges —' He looked to the table. 'Hi, where are they?'

'Whew,' sniffed his mate, 'I can smell 'em.'

I never spoke.

Pongo began to search. He looked high and low, went through my pockets, felt at my brat, but of course he found no trace of an orange. Finally he figured out what must have happened, but even then he couldn't believe it. '*Seventeen* oranges,' he kept murmuring — 'big 'uns at that! — how has he managed it?' But I said nothing. And he couldn't give me in charge, because he had no evidence upon which to commit me — and because I suppose he did not want to be laughed at. So all he could do was to vituperate, while I kept my lips shut tight, and then he had to let me go.

When I told Clem Jones about it he said that I had been very slow; he said that I could have sued Pongo for hundreds of pounds because of wrongful detention, if only I had been quick-witted enough. But I never was a vindictive sort, and anyway, it was days and days before I could stand really still and think things out, because those seventeen oranges — peel, pips, and all — kept working away in my inside something shocking.

BILL NAUGHTON, *The Goal-Keeper's Revenge and Other Stories*

1. Reading for Meaning

(a) Explain why the boy got caught.
(b) Why did the boy keep his mouth shut?
(c) How did Pongo react to the boy's refusal to be interrogated?
(d) What could have happened to the boy if he had been charged?
(e) Why did the boy swallow the pips?
(f) Why didn't the boy chew the oranges?
(g) How was luck on the boy's side?
(h) How did Pongo's mate know that the boy had stolen the oranges?
(i) Why was Pongo amazed when he returned with his mate?
(j) Why couldn't Pongo charge the boy?
(k) What reason could the boy have had for suing Pongo?
(l) Do you admire the boy? Why?
(m) What is your attitude to Pongo?
(n) Why was the boy's experience full of suspense for the reader?

2. Putting the Events in Order

Arrange the following events from the story in the correct order.
(a) Clem Jones said that Pongo could have been sued for hundreds of pounds.
(b) Pongo takes the boy to his cabin.
(c) Pongo and his mate are detained.
(d) A voice in the boy's head tells the boy to eat the oranges.
(e) The boy gets caught because the string of his brat broke.
(f) The oranges made the boy sick for many days afterwards.
(g) The boy decides not to say anything and refuses to be interrogated.
(h) The boy begins to eat the oranges.
(i) Pongo goes off to bring back a colleague to act as a witness.
(j) Pongo's mate can smell the oranges.
(k) There are still three oranges to be eaten.

3. Characters

We learn about a character by what the character says and does. Write the following table into your books and in the blank spaces insert evidence from the story which matches up with each aspect.

	BOY'S CHARACTER TRAIT	EVIDENCE IN THE STORY
(a)	intelligent	
(b)	anxious	
(c)	silent	
(d)	afraid	
(e)	determined	
(f)	calm	

	PONGO'S CHARACTER TRAITS	EVIDENCE IN THE STORY
(g)	diligent (thorough)	
(h)	amazed	
(i)	frustrated	

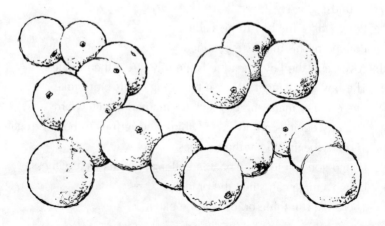

4. In Your Own Words

Explain in your own words the meanings of these expressions from the story.
(a) An example has to be made of somebody.
(b) Anything you say may be used in evidence against you.
(c) I'll bring a colleague as witness.
(d) I was ruined for life.
(e) It's a race against time.
(f) A sort of traffic jam in my oesophagus.
(g) He found no trace of an orange.
(h) The mistake of blabbing.
(i) Those seventeen oranges kept working away in my inside something shocking.
(j) Wrongful detention.

5. Word Forms

Write down these sentences and insert in the blank spaces the correct forms of the words in brackets.
(a) There needed to be two .... to the boy's crime. [witness]
(b) The boy refused to undergo any kind of .... [interrogated]
(c) The boy was placed in a .... predicament. [frightened]
(d) It was .... that the boy had eaten the oranges. [evidence]
(e) The boy had difficulty in .... the last three oranges. [swallowed]
(f) The boy was caught because the oranges .... in his pockets. [bulging]
(g) *Eating the Evidence* is a story full of .... [suspense]
(h) It was more by good .... than good luck that the boy was finally released. [manage]

6. Sentence Correction

Write down these sentences and correct the errors in them as you do so.

(a) There was seventeen oranges in all.
(b) He place them careful on the table.
(c) I didn't say nothing.
(d) Pongo and his mate was detained over checking up on some outgoing wagon.
(e) Each of the oranges were quick ate.
(f) The boy eat the oranges that quickly that he was sick for days.
(g) The boy could of sued Pongo for hundreds of pounds.
(h) Pongo begun to search for the oranges.

7. Spelling

evidence	detention	attitude	bulging
detective	murmuring	suspense	anguish
swallowed	interrogated	managed	escape
witness	suppose	through	frightened
commit	suggesting	carefully	certainly

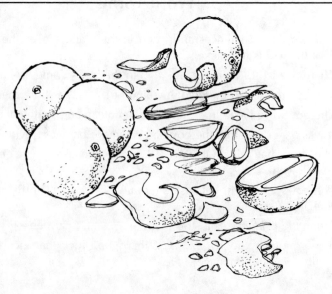

8. Clues

Use the clues to find a spelling word for each of the examples below.

(a) This word is similar in meaning to 'questioned'.
(b) The boy was lucky to .... going to prison.
(c) Unfortunately for Pongo, there was no other .... to the boy's crime.
(d) This word has to do with thinking.
(e) The story has plenty of .... in it.
(f) This word has a married ending.
(g) This word has a masculine beginning.
(h) Any .... would realize the boy had swallowed the oranges.
(i) This word has a painful ending.
(j) The two words have the same number in the middle of them.
(k) This word has a writing instrument in its middle.
(l) This word does not have a smooth ending.

15. The Death of Beowulf

Beowulf, a fearless hero with the strength of thirty men, has killed many monsters throughout the land. In his encounter with the dreaded fire-drake, he is mortally wounded.

But the sound of another voice roused the dragon to yet greater hatred, and the earth groaned and the rocks shivered to his fury, while he drove out blast on blast of searing flame. Wiglaf's shield blackened and flamed like a torch, and he flung the blazing remnant from him and sprang to obey his lord as Beowulf shouted to him, 'Here! Behind my targe — it shall serve to cover us both!' And steady and undismayed they fought on behind the red-hot shield of iron.

But at last, as it came whistling down in mighty blow, Beowulf's sword that had seen the victory in a hundred battles shivered into fragments on the dragon's head.

With a great cry, the King threw the useless hilt away from him, but before he could snatch the saex from his belt, the fire-drake was upon him, rearing up under the flailing darkness of its wings, the poisonous foreclaws slashing at his throat above the golden collar.

In the same instant, while the King's life blood burst out in a red wave, Wiglaf sprang clear of the iron targe and, diving low under the fire-drake, stabbed upward with shortened blade into its scaleless underparts.

A convulsive shudder ran through all the lashing coils of the dragon's body, and instantly the fire began to fade, and as it faded, Beowulf with the last of his battle strength, tore the saex from his belt and hurling himself forward, hacked the great brute almost in two.

The dragon lay dead, with the brightness of its fires darkening upon it. But Beowulf also had got his death hurt, and now as he stood swaying above the huge carcass, his wounds began to burn and swell, the venom from the monster's talons boiled in his breast and all his limbs seemed on fire. Blindly he staggered towards a place where the rocks made a natural couch close beside the cave entrance, and sank down upon it, gasping for air.

ROSEMARY SUTCLIFF, *Dragon Slayer*

1. Reading for Meaning

(a) What did the dragon do when he was angry?
(b) Why was it difficult for Wiglaf and Beowulf to fight the dragon?
(c) What evidence in this story can you find to suggest that Beowulf had been a very successful warrior?
(d) Describe how the dragon was able to deal a death blow to Beowulf.
(e) How does the story show that Beowulf was a particularly strong man?
(f) How was Wiglaf able to kill the dragon?
(g) How did the dragon react to the mortal wound inflicted by Wiglaf?
(h) What did you learn about the character of Wiglaf?
(i) Did you feel any sympathy for Beowulf when he had received his death hurt? Why?
(j) Explain the meaning of these words. (Use the back-of-the-book dictionary if you like.)
  (i) searing
  (ii) convulsive
  (iii) carcass
  (iv) flailing

2. Find-a-Word

Find a word from the passage for each example. The first letter is given to help you.

(a) Another word for fire-drake   d................
(b) This word is the opposite to whitened   b................
(c) This word means little pieces   f................
(d) This word rhymes with moaned   g................
(e) Claws   t................
(f) Handle of a sword   h................
(g) A dagger   s................
(h) Chopped   h................
(i) Shield   t................
(j) Front claws   f................

3. Write Down New Words

Write out the following sentences and for the words in heavy print substitute words of your own that have similar meanings.

(a) Wiglaf's shield blackened and flamed like a torch and he **flung** the blazing remnant from him and sprang to obey his **lord** as Beowulf **shouted** to him, 'Here! Behind my targe — it shall serve to **cover** us both.'

(b) Blindly he **staggered** towards a place where the rocks made a natural **couch** close beside the cave **entrance**, and sank down upon it, **gasping for air**.

(c) In the same **instant**, while the King's life blood **burst** out in a red wave, Wiglaf **sprang clear of** the iron targe and, diving low **under** the fire-drake, **stabbed** upward with shortened blade into its scaleless **underparts**.

4. Opposites

Make up the opposite of these words by adding the prefix 'un' to their beginnings or the suffix 'less' to their endings.

(a)	scale	(c)	cover	(e)	use	(g)	dismayed
(b)	life	(d)	clear	(f)	hurt	(h)	natural

Write down the opposites of these words.

(i)	same	(m)	huge
(j)	shortened	(n)	darkness
(k)	last	(o)	hatred
(l)	victory		

5. Inserting Prepositions

| to | to | on | in | for | for | of | of | of | of | from | with |

Write down the sentences and in the blank spaces put in the correct prepositions from the box.
(a) Some .... the readers of *Dragon Slayer* would be able .... sympathise .... the dragon.
(b) Beowulf aimed .... kill the dragon.
(c) Beowulf and Wiglaf were capable .... great bravery.
(d) Beowulf never complained .... his suffering.
(e) The people in the nearby districts were relying .... Beowulf to kill the dragon.
(f) Beowulf put his trust .... his sword.
(g) Beowulf and Wiglaf had great respect .... the dragon's poisonous talons.
(h) Wiglaf emerged unharmed .... the fight.
(i) Beowulf had a reputation .... bravery.
(j) Beowulf became a victim .... the dragon's poisonous talons.

6. Spelling Words

poisonous	entrance	instantly
carcass	remnant	convulsive
stagger	undismayed	whistling
natural	shudder	shivered
strength	fragments	venom

All the examples in Ex. 7 are based on the spelling words.

7. Use the Clues

(a) Find a word in the box that could be applied to a drunk person.
(b) Write down two of the spelling words that are often used with harmful snakes.
(c) Write down a verb coming from the word 'entrance'.
(d) Find a spelling word that is opposite to 'weakness'.
(e) Find a spelling word meaning 'remainder'.
(f) This spelling word ends with a colour.
(g) This spelling word has a month of the year in it.
(h) This spelling word has the opposite of 'women' in the middle.
(i) This spelling word rhymes with length.
(j) This spelling word begins with an animal.

8. Completing the Sentences

Complete these sentences using your knowledge of the story.

(a) The dragon's fire began to fade when ....
(b) Beowulf probably would not have been killed if ....
(c) Beowulf hacked the dragon almost in two after ....
(d) Wiglaf, whose .... stabbed the dragon in its scaleless underparts.
(e) The dragon slashed at Beowulf's throat with its foreclaws, which ....
(f) Beowulf's wounds began to burn and swell because ....
(g) Beowulf's sword was shattered when ....
(h) Beowulf, whose .... staggered towards a couch of stone.

16. The World's Worst Whinger

Ever met a full time grumbler? If you have, you won't have any trouble in recognizing the long-faced character in this yarn. Billy Borker tells it over a drink with a mate in the pub . . .

What would be the best Australian story you ever heard?

Well, I reckon the most fair dinkum Australian story ever told was about the World's Worst Whinger. I call it: 'How would I be?'

Have another drink and tell me about it.

I don't mind if I do. I first met this bloke — the World's Worst Whinger — in a shearing shed in Queensland during the Depression. I asked him an innocent question: 'How would you be?' Well, he dropped the sheep he was shearing, spat, and fixed me with a pair of bitter eyes and he says: 'How would I be? How would you expect me to be? Get a load of me, will you? Dags on every inch of me hide; drinking me own sweat; swallowing dirt with every breath I breathe; shearing sheep that should have been dogs' meat years ago; working for the lousiest boss in Australia; frightened to leave because the old woman's looking for me in Brisbane with a maintenance order. How would I be? I haven't tasted beer for weeks and the last glass I had was knocked over by some clumsy coot before I finished it.'

He must have been a whinger, all right.

The world's worst, like I told you. Next time I met him he was in an army camp in Melbourne. He'd joined the A.I.F. 'How would you be?' I asked him. 'How would I be? Get a load of this outfit. Look at me flamin' hat. Size nine and a half and I take six and a half. Get an eyeful of these strides — you could hide a blasted brewery horse in the seat of them and still have room for me. And get on to these boots, will yer? There's enough leather in 'em to make a full set of harness. And some idiot brass-hat told me this was a man's outfit. How would I be? How would you *expect* me to be?'

Is this story true?

True? Well most of my stories are true but this one, you might say it's truer than true. I met him next in Tobruk. He was sitting on a box, tin hat over one eye, cigarette butt dangling from his bottom lip, rifle leaning on one knee, cleaning his finger nails with his bayonet. I should have known better but I asked him: 'How would you be, Dig?' He swallowed his cigarette butt and stared at me with a malevolent eye. 'How would I be? How would I be? How would you expect me to be? Shot at by every Fritz in Africa; eating sand with every meal; flies in me eyes; frightened to go to sleep; expecting to die in this God-forsaken place. And you ask me *how would I be?*

Did you ever meet him again?

No, he was killed in Tobruk, as a matter of fact.

Well, one thing, he wouldn't do any more whingeing, poor devil.

You know, I dreamt about him the other night.

Yeh?

Yeh. I dreamt I died and went to Heaven. It was as clear as on a television screen. I saw him there in my dream and I asked: 'How would you be?' He eyed me with an angelic expression and he says; 'How would I be? Get an eyeful of this night-gown, will yer? A man trips over it fifty times a day and takes ten minutes to lift it to scratch his knee. And take a gander at me right wing, feathers falling out of it, a man must be moulting. Cast your eyes over this halo; only me big ears keep the rotten thing on me skull. And just take a Captain Cook at this harp, five strings missing and there's band practice in five minutes. *How would I be? you ask. How would you expect a man to bloody well be?'*

A good story. Yes, a beauty.

The most fair dinkum Australian story ever told . . .

FRANK HARDY, *The Yarns of Billy Borker*

1. Reading for Meaning

(a) Suggest why the whinger was the world's worst.
(b) How do we know that the whinger's marriage was in trouble?
(c) Which of the whinger's exaggerations about his army uniform is the most unlikely?
(d) The sentence that begins, 'Well, most of my stories . . .' contains an impossibility. What is it?
(e) Why was Tobruk a God-forsaken place?
(f) Which of the whinger's whinges in Tobruk comes true?

The World's Worst Whinger

(g) How does the dream resemble a television screen?
(h) 'He eyed me with *an angelic expression* . . .' Why is the phrase in italics particularly appropriate (fitting)?
(i) Of all the whinger's whinges about heaven, which one do you think is the most humorous? Why?
(j) Do you think this is a good Australian story? Why?

2. Vocabulary Crossword

Test your knowledge of some of the most interesting words in *The World's Worst Whinger* by drawing the crossword in your workbook and filling it in. All the clues refer to words in the story.

Across
1 'Care' beginning with 'm'
3 A pointed blade fixed to a rifle
5 Losing fur or feathers
6 An evil creature from hell
8 The used end of a cigarette
9 A good look
11 Encloses the brain

Down
2 Leather gear used for controlling a horse
4 'Evil' beginning with 'm'
7 Yet, in the sense of 'continuing'
8 A place where beer is made
10 Awkward; not skilful or agile
12 A circle of light round the head, showing goodness

3. Slang Slot

Much of the story's special Australian flavour is gained by using slang words or phrases. Match up slang words or phrases on the left with common English words or phrases on the right.

	SLANG	COMMON ENGLISH
(a)	fair dinkum	look
(b)	whinger	trousers
(c)	lousiest	skin
(d)	old woman	true, genuine
(e)	coot	look
(f)	outfit	a person who complains a lot
(g)	strides	man
(h)	brass-hat	organization
(i)	gander	high ranking officer
(j)	Captain Cook	a silly individual
(k)	hide	mother
(l)	bloke	miserly, mean, very bad

4. Sizing Up Adjectives

Adjectives usually have three forms : **positive, comparative, superlative.**

    small   smaller   smallest

Some adjectives do it this way:

    difficult   more difficult   most difficult

On the other hand, a few adjectives are *irregular* and have different forms for their positive, comparative and superlative.

    little   less   least

The World's Worst Whinger

In 'The World's Worst Whinger', adjectives in the superlative are a specialty — as they would be in any yarn that deals with exaggeration. Copy the table into your workbook and fill it in for all the adjectives.

	POSITIVE	COMPARATIVE	SUPERLATIVE
(a)			best
(b)	big		
(c)		harder	
(d)			worst
(e)		longer	
(f)	beautiful		
(g)			most
(h)	cautious		
(i)			lousiest
(j)	clumsy		
(k)	talkative		
(l)		clearer	

Why is it that, in a strictly literal sense, neither 'full' nor 'true' can be put into the comparative or the superlative? Think of a few examples that go *against* this 'rule', however, and explain why such exceptions 'get away with it'.

5. Apostrophes (no need to whinge about them!)

Several rules for using the apostrophe (') are illustrated in the story.

• **Using the Apostrophe to Show Possession**
To show the singular possessive form of a noun, add **'s** to the noun.
  The whinger**'s** greatest trouble was that he could never be happy.
To show the plural possessive form of a noun whose plural ends in **'s'**, add only an **'**.
  Diggers**'** helmets were called 'tin hats'.

Put in the apostrophes:

(a) Worlds worst
(b) Should have been dogs meat
(c) A brass-hats comment
(d) A mans outfit
(e) Angels harps
(f) Five minutes worth of band practice
(g) A coots clumsy move
(h) This rifles bayonet
(i) Shearers troubles
(j) A brewery horses hiding place.

• **Using Apostrophes for Contractions**
When one or two words are contracted or shortened, an apostrophe is used to show where sounds or letters have been removed.
  Should not — shouldn't

Make contractions of the following words, putting in apostrophes where needed:

(k) he is
(l) have not
(m) there is
(n) do not
(o) would not
(p) them
(q) flaming

(r) you are
(s) is not
(t) we will
(u) need not
(v) it is
(w) she is
(x) I have

Does the apostrophe show possession or contraction in the clause 'because the old woman's looking for me . . .'?

6. Vanished Vowels

Add vowels (a,e,i,o,u) to the collections of consonants (all the letters of the alphabet that are not vowels) below to form words from the passage. All the words denote things used or experienced by the whinger. Brief clues are given.

(a)	hl	Heavenly object
(b)	rfl	Weapon
(c)	ml	Something to eat
(d)	fls	Winged pests
(e)	hrp	Stringed instrument
(f)	bx	Something to sit on
(g)	brth	Essential for life
(h)	br	A strong drink
(i)	drm	Occurs in sleep
(j)	lthr	Animal product
(k)	nls	On the fingers
(l)	ys	In the head
(m)	mt	A kind of food
(n)	lp	On the face
(o)	swt	Produced by the body
(p)	hd	On the body
(q)	cmp	A place to stay
(r)	hrs	A big animal
(s)	ers	On the head
(t)	bnd	Musical group

17. The Hiding Place

'The Silver Sword' is the story of three children, Ruth, Edek and Bronia Balicki and their efforts to find their parents in Nazi-occupied Europe. This passage describes the narrow escape of their father from death at the hands of his Nazi pursuers.

Suddenly there was a loud bang on the door. Was it a search party? If so, why had the old man given no warning?

A voice called out in German.

There was not time to escape to the woodshed.

'Quick — up there!' The old woman pointed up the chimney. 'There's an opening on the right, half-way up.'

Joseph dived into the hearth and hauled himself up over the iron spit. The fire was only smouldering and there was not much smoke. He had not found the opening when the door burst open and two soldiers came in. While they searched the room, he stood very still, his legs astride the chimney. He wanted to cough. He thought his lungs would burst.

Suddenly a head peered up the chimney. It was the old woman, 'They've gone upstairs,' she said. 'But don't come down yet.'

She showed him where the opening was. He crept inside, coughing. He could see the sky through the wide chimney top above him.

He was congratulating himself on his good luck when he heard the soldiers return to the room below. With difficulty he controlled his cough.

'What about the chimney? said a German voice. 'Plenty of room to hide up there.'

'Plenty of soot too,' said the other soldier. 'Your uniform's older than mine. What about you going up?'

'Not likely.'

'Then we'll send a couple of bullets up for luck.'

Two ear-splitting explosions. It seemed as if the whole chalet was falling down. Joseph clung on to his perch. There was a great tumbling about his ears. He clung and clung and clung — till his fingers were torn from their grip, and he fell.

When he came to his senses, he was lying on the floor. The old woman was bending over him, washing his face with cold water.

'It's all right — they've gone,' she said. 'The fall of soot saved you. The soldiers ran for it when the soot came down. They were afraid for their uniforms.'

IAN SERRAILLIER, *The Silver Sword*

1. Reading for Meaning

(a) Why wasn't Joseph able to escape to the woodshed?
(b) How did the old woman react to the banging on the door?
(c) Why was Joseph able to hide in the chimney?
(d) Why didn't the German soldiers go up the chimney?
(e) 'He clung and clung and clung' By repeating 'clung', what is the writer telling the reader?
(f) Why did it seem 'as though the whole chalet was falling down'?
(g) Why did the fall of soot save Joseph?
(h) What did you learn about the character of the old woman?
(i) What did you learn about the character of Joseph?
(j) Explain the meaning of these words. (You may like to use the back-of-the-book dictionary to help you.)

   (i) hearth   (ii) smouldering
   (iii) peered   (iv) hauled
   (v) chalet   (vi) astride

2. Forming New Words

Fill in the gaps and make up new words based on words in the story.

(a) sense   sens __ bl __
                 sens __ t __ __ __
(b) control   controll __ __
                 controll __ __ __ __
                 controll __ __ g
(c) open   open __
                 open __ __
                 open __ __ __

(d) explode   explos _ _ _
               explod _ _
               explos _ v _ _ _
               explos _ _ n
(e) congratulate   congratulat _ _
                   congratulat _ _ _
                   congratulat _ _ _ s
                   congratulat _ _ g

3. Completing the Verb Table

Complete the following table by inserting verbs of either present or past time. The first one has been done for you. Often the answer is to be found in the story.

	PRESENT	PAST
	He clings	He clung
(a)		He sent
(b)	He creeps	
(c)		He tore
(d)	He runs	
(e)	He lies (down)	
(f)		He fell
(g)	He peers	
(h)		He tumbled
(i)	He stands	
(j)	He thinks	
(k)	He bends	

4. Giving Variety to Sentences

Rewrite each of the following sentences as instructed.

- (a) (i) It seemed as if the whole chalet was falling down.
  - (ii) The whole chalet ....
- (b) (i) Joseph dived into the hearth and hauled himself up over the iron spit.
  - (ii) Joseph, diving ....
- (c) (i) The fire was only smouldering and there was not much smoke.
  - (ii) There was not much smoke because ....
- (d) (i) Suddenly a head peered up the chimney.
  - (ii) Up the chimney ....
- (e) (i) 'They've gone upstairs,' she said.
  - (ii) She said that ....
- (f) (i) The fall of soot saved you.
  - (ii) You were saved ....

5. Putting the Words Back Together

Match up the two columns to make words from the story. If you do it successfully, you'll have a complete match up.

(a)	re	ions
(b)	like	y
(c)	old	ly
(d)	cough	er
(e)	in	turn
(f)	difficult	ing
(g)	sold	forms
(h)	bull	stairs
(i)	uni	self
(j)	explos	ier
(k)	up	ets
(l)	him	side

The Hiding Place 129

6. Changing the Verbs to Present Time

'She showed him where the opening was' is a sentence written in past time. If you write the sentence in present time, it becomes: 'She shows (is showing) him where the opening is'.

Change each of these sentences to present time.
(a) Suddenly there was a bang on the door.
(b) He thought his lungs would burst.
(c) Was it a search party?
(d) He could see the sky through the wide chimney above him.
(e) His fingers were torn from their grip.
(f) They were afraid for their uniforms.
(g) He wanted to cough.
(h) A voice called out in German.

7. Forming Plurals

Form the plurals of the words below. Most of them come from the story.

chimney	church	piano
difficulty	chief	bullet
woman	uniform	voice
warning	knife	sky
man	explosion	perch
search	soldier	door
party	potato	match

8. Helping the Conjunctions

The words in heavy type are conjunctions. Using your knowledge of the story, complete the sentences starting from the conjunctions.
(a) Joseph fell from the perch **when** ....
(b) The old lady told Joseph not to come down **because** ....
(c) The soldiers would have found Joseph **if** ....
(d) The soldiers ran for it **when** ....
(e) The old lady helped Joseph **although** ....
(f) The old lady told Joseph he was safe **after** ....

THE BRUMBY

A Puffin Book

18. A Brumby Fight

Brumby is a wild Australian stallion, and in this extract a fight between rival stallions is graphically described.

Then each fighter worked himself up into the required pitch of fury. Dust billowed upwards from their pawing hooves, making gauzy, golden globes about them in the sunlight, blurring the outlines of their two bodies.

Like a white flame blown by a gust of wind, the silver horse sprang from his misty covering towards the other, and the chestnut met him with snapping teeth, flint-edged hooves and eyes red with hate.

The tangled manes tossed and teeth clashed as the horses reared chest to chest, heads darting, front hooves striking, their movements a gigantic and deadly dance. In the dusty nimbus they spun around, wrestling and weaving, hooves smashed against muscled bodies, hides were torn and blood spurted.

The fighting of bulls is a thing of weight and brute courage, it is charged with primeval brutality and noise. The fighting of stallions is a far more terrible thing, for it brings pride to the kill, intelligence and will and a refusal to accept defeat even in the ultimate agony of being beaten down, driven off, or killed.

Blood poured down Brumby's sides and from his neck the flesh hung down in shredded red ribbons. Things might have gone badly for him but for an accidental blow that happened in the wheeling and twisting of the other's body. The sharp edge of his hoof struck against the stifle of the older horse, pulping the bone and causing him to arch his loins in agony above his useless leg.

This was Brumby's chance and he took it, charging in with his great weight, screaming, biting, kicking. The other stallion staggered on three legs then overbalanced and fell. In an instant Brumby was on him, hooves pounding the life from his body, while his great teeth instinctively tore at his throat and his life ebbed away.

Rage died down in the victorious stallion. He stood above his fallen enemy, head high, neck arched, his own blood dripping downwards and mingling with his foe's. The wildness died from his eyes and his laboured breathing became calmer. Throwing his head high he whinnied his victory, giving out a sound as different as is the snarl of a fighting dog from the purr of a contented cat. He wheeled and trotted, stepping high, and going towards the stranger's mares he drove them into line and sent them towards his own waiting mares.

They, in a world where might is right, probably gave no thought to their fallen leader, but transferred their allegiance to his skill, his courage which had kept them free, his cunning which kept them fed and watered, to his successor. Some day, in his turn, he might yet lose them to another stallion, perhaps a grandson of his own in all the power and beauty of youth.

M. E. PATCHETT, *The Brumby*

1. Reading for Meaning

(a) What did each of the stallions need to do before the fight could begin?

(b) The hooves of the fighting stallions produce strange shapes in the air.
  (i) What are the shapes like?
  (ii) What are they made of?

(c) Find a comparison in which the silver horse is likened to something else.

(d) What emotion is felt by the chestnut stallion and how do we know of its existence?

(e) A 'gigantic and deadly dance'. These words are part of a comparison. What is the other part?

(f) Give four reasons why the fighting of stallions is more terrible than the fighting of bulls.

(g) One incident in the struggle marks a turning point in favour of Brumby. What is the incident?

(h) Explain the meaning of the words, 'in a world where might is right'.

(i) What advantages did the mares gain from accepting the leadership of a stallion?

(j) There is the suggestion that some day the Brumby, in his turn, might be defeated by another stallion. What quality in another stallion might overcome Brumby?

2. Dictionary, Take Ten

Look up in the back-of-the-book dictionary these ten words from the passage:

billowed	instinctively
nimbus	ebbed
primeval	might
ultimate	allegiance
stifle	successor

Now, rewrite the following sentences choosing, as you go, the word from among the ten that will complete the sense of each sentence.

(a) They transferred their .... to his skill and his courage.
(b) Brumby's great teeth .... tore at his throat.
(c) Dust .... upwards from their pawing hooves.
(d) The fighting of bulls is charged with .... brutality and noise.
(e) The sharp edge of his hoof struck against the .... of the older horse.
(f) The brumby became the chestnut's ....
(g) In the dusty .... they spun around, wrestling and weaving.
(h) The life of the chestnut .... away.
(i) In a world where .... is right, the mares probably gave no thought to their fallen leader.
(j) Fighting stallions often refuse to accept defeat even in the .... agony of being beaten down, driven off, or killed.

3. Colour and Sound

In such a dramatic description of a fight you'd naturally expect to find words of colour and sound.

Write down 5 words of colour and 6 of noise from the passage. The first letters and spaces are supplied to help you.

	COLOUR WORDS		SOUND WORDS
(a)	s_ _ _ _ _ _	(e)	p_ _ _ _
(b)	c_ _ _ _ _ _ _	(f)	w_ _ _ _ _ _
(c)	r_ _	(g)	n_ _ _ _
(d)	g_ _ _ _ _	(h)	c_ _ _ _ _ _

4. Abstract Nouns

Abstract nouns are words that name qualities or states of mind, or whatever it is that can be talked about but cannot be touched, e.g. fear.

In the fight between the stallions, Mary Patchett uses abstract nouns to reveal qualities in the combatants and their surroundings.

Supply the abstract noun, given another part of speech (e.g. fearful — **fear**).

All the abstract nouns you are asked to find are in the passage.

	WORD	ABSTRACT NOUN
(a)	furious	
(b)	hating	
(c)	brutal	
(d)	proud	
(e)	intelligent	
(f)	willed	
(g)	defeating	
(h)	victorious	
(i)	wild	
(j)	courageous	
(k)	powerful	
(l)	skilled	
(m)	beautiful	
(n)	living	

A Brumby Fight 135

5. Variety

Strong verbs and powerful adjectives are at work in the fight between the stallions.

Notice, as you work the exercise that follows, how many different verbs and adjectives are used. Sometimes the same noun appears in different places in the passage with a variety of verbs and adjectives. Such variety keeps a reader's interest alive.

Look at the drawing of the fight. Write down in your workbook the strong verbs and powerful adjectives that go with the nouns. Check back with the passage to make sure you've got them right.

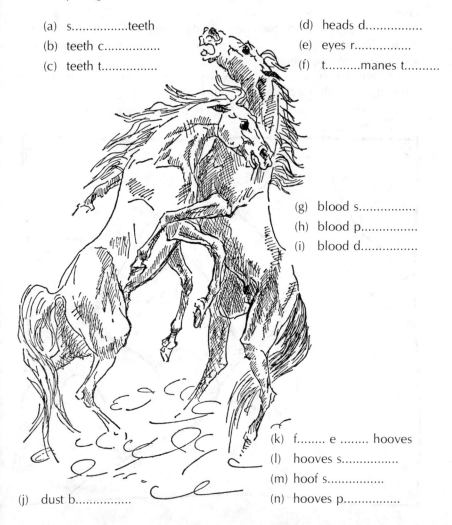

(a) s................teeth
(b) teeth c................
(c) teeth t................
(d) heads d................
(e) eyes r................
(f) t.........manes t.........
(g) blood s................
(h) blood p................
(i) blood d................
(j) dust b................
(k) f........ e .... hooves
(l) hooves s................
(m) hoof s................
(n) hooves p................

136 Word Skills One

6. Round Up the Runaways

Ten runaway nouns and adjectives are missing from the summary of 'The Brumby'. However, they are all gathered in the 'hills'.

Rewrite the passage putting in the nouns and adjectives where they will fit and complete the sense of the sentences.

The Brumby

The Brumby of this story was a wild .... stallion, by chance born near the home of a .... boy and capturing his .... with such intensity that he could think and dream of nothing but one day building up a .... of sturdy .... brumbies.

But to the Australian stockmen among whom he lived all brumbies were wild, vicious, ... animals fit only to be hunted, and young Joey had to endure seeing his .... foal grow up into a .... outlaw and finally a .... Nevertheless his dream comes true in the end, although not quite as he'd imagined it.

This book has wonderful .... of the Australian bush, and of the ways of its men and animals.

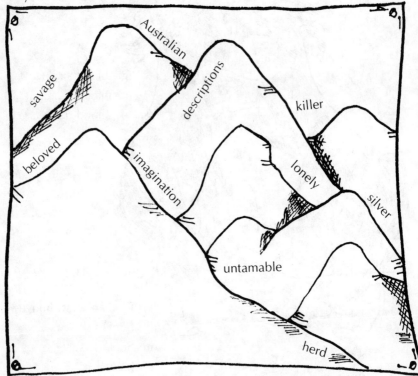

7. Alliteration

Alliteration is a figure of speech.

In alliteration, the emphasis is on sound. There is a repetition (a repeating) of the same consonant sounds that begin a 'run' of words. Repetition often calls attention to a 'run' of words, and gives a certain quality to them.

    cruel **c**awing **c**rows. (Notice the harshness.)

Now look through the passage and find various examples of alliteration. To help you, you are given the paragraph where the alliteration is to be found and the letter that begins each word of the alliteration. As you find each example of alliteration, write it down in your workbook. Here's an example:

(a) Paragraph 2 [S]   *the silver horse sprang*
(b) Paragraph 1 [G]   ....
(c) Paragraph 3 [T]   the ....
(d) Paragraph 3 [D]   ....
(e) Paragraph 3 [W]   ....
(f) Paragraph 5 [R]   in sh..... ....
(g) Paragraph 5 [S]   the ....
(h) Paragraph 6 [T]   ....
(i) Paragraph 7 [D]   ....
(j) Paragraph 7 [C]   a ....

19. Pursuit by a Grizzly Bear

After the death of his parents, thirteen-year-old John Sager sets out with his six younger brothers and sisters to keep faith with his father's dream of crossing to Oregon. Based on the true-life story of John Sager, this book recounts their appalling hardships.

There, in an inlet in the undergrowth, on a little sandy beach, an enormous bear with three young lay basking in the sun.

Louise's heart stood still; she caught her breath. Her only thought was to get away, noiselessly, without the bear noticing. But she stood there as though paralysed, she could not move for sheer fright.

A branch snapped. Slowly the bear lifted its head, looked round . . .

Louise dropped the waterskins and ran, as fast as her bare feet could carry her. Behind her, the bear came splashing across the river, through the shallow water.

John was still busy with the antelope, when he suddenly heard a penetrating scream. Another, and yet another — close at hand now. They came from the direction of the river — it could only be Louise. There she was — screaming. Her arms stretched out in front of her, she came tearing along in the strange green twilight between the willow shrubs. Behind her came a sound of cracking and snapping. . .

It was a bear, a huge, reddish-brown grizzly bear, whose ungainly body thrashed along at breakneck speed through the green tunnel of the path, which was much too narrow for it. The brute was no more than ten feet away from Louise; a terrifying snarl came from its throat.

Wagh! Savagely it launched itself forward; Louise had reached the open space.

'John,' she cried, 'help me!'

The boy already had his gun to his shoulder, but he trembled, he did not dare to shoot yet.

The she-bear was momentarily dazed by the sharper light, perhaps also by the camp fire, and confused by the many possibilities she saw there, after first having thought of only Louise as prey.

She stopped for a second, reared up on her hind legs, and mowed the air with her formidable paws with their great, sharp claws — a hairy monster ready for the attack.

And now two young bears appeared behind her. Growling, with upper lips bared in a snarl, and white teeth, heavy and woolly, they lurched along behind their mother. Just as the bear had been put out by the sight of the many children, so was John taken aback by the danger of three bears.

He only had one shot in his gun.

He did his utmost to control himself, he bit his tongue between his teeth, he *had* to save the children.

But he was not alone.

He fired . . . and at the same moment Oscar, the wolf dog, shot forward, and flew straight at the great bear's shaggy throat, bit tightly into it, and would not be shaken off.

The bear tottered. She had been hit; where, John did not know.

Francis fired his two pistols, one after the other.

A bullet struck the bear's left ear; dark red blood started to drip down its terrifying head. The monster roared, tried to get rid of the dog; there was a storm of white fangs and curving paws with vicious yellow talons, lightning swings, blows and growls. The dog yelped, but held on; the movements of the bear became more sluggish.

The animal reared up. Oscar hung on to her throat; blood trickled to the ground from an open gash on his back.

Francis thrust a fresh rifle into John's hands and he fired a second shot, right between the little flashing eyes. The bear growled, gurgled, and fell forward.

A. RUTGERS VAN DER LOEFF, *Children on the Oregon Trail*

1. Reading for Meaning

(a) When Louise first saw the bear she was unable to move because
   (i) the waterskins were too heavy to carry.
   (ii) she knew if she tried she would make a noise.
   (iii) she was unsure how dangerous it might be.
   (iv) she was frozen with fear.

(b) John did not dare fire at first because
   (i) he was afraid of hitting Louise.
   (ii) he knew that wounding the bear would make it much more dangerous.
   (iii) he was frightened of the bear.
   (iv) the bear was still too far away.

(c) The fact that the grizzly hesitated when it saw the other children shows that
   (i) it was not as fierce as it first seemed.
   (ii) it was able to sense danger.
   (iii) for a moment it was confused by what it saw.
   (iv) it was almost ready to give up the chase.

(d) The bear's flight after Louise was
   (i) slow, very noisy and awkward.
   (ii) surprisingly agile, noisy and swift.
   (iii) swift, fairly noiseless and awkward.
   (iv) awkward, very noisy and very fast.

(e) John was taken aback at the sight of the young bears because
   (i) he knew that a young bear is even more dangerous than its parent.
   (ii) he knew he could only shoot one bear with his rifle.
   (iii) the sight was unexpected and he was unsure what to do.
   (iv) he did not want to have to shoot the young bears.

(f) Francis
   (i) was older than John.
   (ii) hit the bear's ear with a pistol shot.
   (iii) fired the shot that finally killed the grizzly.
   (iv) was too young to fire a rifle.

(g) 'But he was not alone.' In this sentence the author is referring particularly to the presence of
   (i) Oscar, the wolf dog.
   (ii) Francis.
   (iii) God.
   (iv) the other children.

(h) Oscar flew at the bear's throat because
   (i) he was specially trained to attack grizzlies.
   (ii) retreat was impossible with the bush all around them.
   (iii) he could see that John was not sure what to do.
   (iv) he knew he had to protect the children.

2. Matching Beginnings and Endings

Match the beginnings of sentences from the left-hand column with their correct endings from the right-hand column.

	BEGINNING	ENDING
(a)	Another, and yet another — ...	... the movements of the bear became more sluggish.
(b)	Her arms stretched out in front of her ...	... without the bear noticing.
(c)	The dog yelped, but held on; ...	... he *had* to save the children.
(d)	The boy already had his gun to his shoulder, but he trembled, ...	... close at hand now.
(e)	Growling, with upper lips bared in a snarl, and white teeth, heavy and woolly, ...	... Louise had reached the open space.
(f)	He did his utmost to control himself, he bit his tongue between his teeth, ...	... she came tearing along in the strange green twilight between the willow shrubs.
(g)	Francis thrust a fresh rifle into John's hands ...	... when he suddenly heard a penetrating scream.
(h)	Her only thought was to get away, noiselessly, ...	... and he fired a second shot, right between the little flashing eyes.
(i)	Savagely it launched itself forward; ...	... he did not dare to shoot yet.
(j)	John was still busy with the antelope, ...	... they lurched along behind their mother.

3. What Does It Mean?

Below are words selected from the passage. Four possible meanings surround each word. Your task is to choose the correct meaning in each case. If you are uncertain, refer to the dictionary at the back of the book.

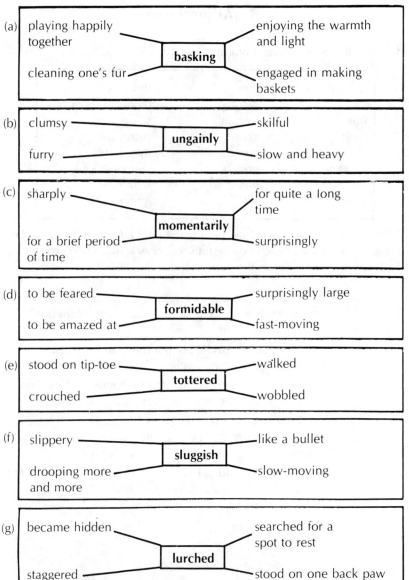

4. In Sentences

To show that you thoroughly understand the meaning of each of the words in Exercise 3, use each one in a sentence.

5. Adjectives

Here is a list of adjectives from the passage.

second	little	flashing
vicious	woolly	reddish-brown
fresh	ungainly	sharp
hind	great	heavy
white	curving	formidable
breakneck	grizzly	yellow
huge	white	lightning
upper		green

Rewrite the sentences below, putting the right adjectives from the box in the blank spaces. When you've finished, check your efforts by finding the complete sentences in the passage.

(a) It was a bear, a ...., ... bear, whose .... body thrashed along at .... speed through the .... tunnel of the path.

(b) Growling, with .... lips bared in a snarl, and .... teeth, ... and ...., they lurched along behind their mother.

(c) Francis thrust a .... rifle into John's hands and he fired a .... shot, right between the .... eyes.

(d) She stopped for a second, reared up on her .... legs, and mowed the air with her .... paws with their ...., ... claws.

(e) The monster roared, tried to get rid of the dog; there was a storm of .... fangs and .... paws with .... talons, ... swings, blows and growls.

6. Antonyms

Find antonyms (words opposite in meaning) for the following words from the extract. The first one has been done for you.

	WORD	ANTONYM
	enormous	tiny
(a)	young	
(b)	noiselessly	
(c)	slowly	
(d)	shallow	
(e)	sound	
(f)	narrow	
(g)	open	
(h)	first	
(i)	hind	
(j)	sharp	
(k)	attack	
(l)	hairy	
(m)	heavy	
(n)	tightly	
(o)	fresh	
(p)	little	
(q)	forward	

My Side of the Mountain

JEAN GEORGE

20. Frightful the Falcon

Sam Gribley ran away from his family's flat in New York to the Catskill Mountains. All he took with him was a penknife, a ball of string, an axe and forty dollars.

After splashing across the stream in the shallow, I stood at the bottom of the cliff and wondered how on earth I was going to climb the sheer wall.

I wanted a falcon so badly, however, that I dug in with my toes and hands and started up. The first part was easy; it was not too steep. When I thought I was stuck, I found a little ledge and shinnied up to it.

I was high, and when I looked down, the stream spun. I decided not to look down any more. I edged up to another ledge, and lay down on it to catch my breath. I was shaking from exertion and I was tired.

I looked up to see how much higher I had to go when my hand touched something moist. I pulled it back and saw that it was white — bird droppings. Then I saw them. Almost where my hand had been sat three fuzzy whitish-grey birds. Their wide-open mouths gave them a startled look.

'Oh, hello, hello,' I said. 'You are cute.'

When I spoke, all three blinked at once. All three heads turned and followed my hand as I swung it up and towards them. All three watched my hand with opened mouths. They were marvellous. I chuckled. But I couldn't reach them.

I wormed forward, and *wham!* — something hit my shoulder. It hurt. I turned my head to see the big female. She had bitten me. She winged out, banked, and started back for another strike.

Now I was scared, for I was sure she would cut me wide open. With sudden nerve, I stood up, stepped forward, and picked up the biggest of the nestlings. The females are bigger than the males. They are the 'falcons'. They are the pride of kings. I tucked her in my sweater and leaned against the cliff, facing the bullet-like dive of the falcon. I threw out my foot as she struck, and the sole of my tennis shoe took the blow.

The female was now gathering speed for another attack, and when I say speed, I mean 50 to 60 miles an hour. I could see myself battered and torn, lying in the valley below, and I said to myself, 'Sam Gribley, you had better get down from here like a rabbit.'

I jumped to the ledge below, found it was really quite wide, slid on the seat of my pants to the next ledge, and stopped. The hawk apparently couldn't count. She did not know I had a youngster, for she checked her nest, saw the open mouths, and then she forgot me.

I scrambled to the river bed somehow, being very careful not to hurt the hot fuzzy body that was against my own. However, Frightful, as I called her right then and there because of the difficulties we had had in getting together, did not think so gently of me. She dug her talons into my skin to brace herself during the bumpy ride to the ground.

I stumbled to the stream, placed her in a nest of buttercups, and dropped beside her. I fell asleep.

When I awoke my eyes opened on two grey eyes in a white tousled head. Small pinfeathers were sticking out of the soft down, like feathers in an Indian quiver. The big blue beak curled down in a snarl and up in a smile.

'Oh, Frightful,' I said, 'you are a raving beauty.'

JEAN GEORGE, *My Side of the Mountain*

1. Reading for Meaning

(a) Account for the fact that 'the stream spun' when Sam looked down.
(b) What was the first clue Sam detected that made him realize he was near a nest?
(c) What standard did Sam use in deciding which baby falcon he would take? Why did he use this standard?
(d) From each of the alternatives, pick the one nearest in meaning to the first word:
   (i) *exertion*: fear, nervousness, effort, energy
   (ii) *banked*: turned, climbed, soared, glided
   (iii) *talons*: abilities, wings, feet, claws
   (iv) *(to) brace*: tie, cheer, strengthen, revenge
(e) What are the two parts of the body where Sam was hit by the diving falcon?
(f) Explain why the dive of an adult falcon can be described as 'bullet-like'.
(g) How does Sam account for the mother falcon leaving him alone after he has descended some distance from the nest?
(h) Explain why Sam had to be very careful as he completed the climb back down to the river.
(i) What evidence is there for the fact that Sam was worn out by his climb?
(j) By referring to what happens in the extract, write three sentences about the kind of person Sam is.

2. 'Bird' Verbs

Use a suitable part of each of the 'bird' verbs in the brackets to fill the blanks and complete the following passage.

The falcon .... [to preen] herself, fluffing her feathers and turning her head. Then .... [to soar] aloft, she began to search for prey. .... [to glide] and .... [to bank], she .... [to wing] her way across the countryside. Seeing a tiny movement she .... [to hover] for a split second, then .... [to drop]. .... [to dive] like a flash, she .... [to strike] at a young rabbit, caught it in her talons and, as quickly as she had come, ... [to swoop] away with her prey.

3. Criss-Crossword

The solution to each of the clues below is a word from the extract. Draw up the criss-crossword in your exercise book, and solve the clues.

Across

1. Climbed on hands and knees
2. The smaller of the two falcon sexes
3. The baby falcon was tucked in this
4. What the baby falcon used to brace herself

Down

5. Number of baby falcons found
6. A person who would be proud to have a falcon
7. Where the mother falcon first hit the boy
8. This caused the boy to shake during the climb
9. The boy's name (backwards)
10. This spun when the boy looked down

4. Short and Long Sentences

The length of sentences can be varied fairly easily. A long sentence can be broken down into short sentences.
- When I thought I was stuck, I found a little ledge and shinnied up to it.
- I thought I was stuck. I found a little ledge. I shinnied up to it.

On the other hand, short sentences can be joined to make one longer sentence.
- They were marvellous. I chuckled. But I couldn't reach them.
- They were so marvellous that I chuckled, but I still couldn't reach them.

Break each of the following sentences down into several short sentences.

(a) I was high, and when I looked down, the stream spun.
(b) With sudden nerve, I stood up, stepped forward, and picked up the biggest of the nestlings.
(c) I tucked her in my sweater and leaned against the cliff, facing the bulletlike dive of the falcon.
(d) I jumped to the ledge below, found it was really quite wide, slid on the seat of my pants to the next ledge, and stopped.
(e) She did not know I had a youngster, for she checked her nest, saw the open mouths, and then she forgot me.

Now join the following short sentences into one long sentence in each case.

(f) I wormed forward, and *wham!* — something hit my shoulder. It hurt.
(g) I turned to see the big female. She had bitten me.
(h) The females are bigger than the males. They are the 'falcons'. They are the pride of kings.
(i) I stumbled to the stream, placed her in a nest of buttercups and dropped beside her. I fell asleep.

Discuss:
(j) Why do writers vary the length of their sentences?
(k) What emotions or moods can be created by the use of long, complex sentences?
(l) What emotions or moods can be created by the use of short sentences?

5. Adults and Youngsters

In the extract, a baby falcon is spoken of as a 'nestling'. Match the 'youngsters' from the left-hand column with their adults in the right-hand column.

	ADULTS	YOUNGSTERS
(a)	deer	foal
(b)	lion	chicken
(c)	horse	fawn
(d)	kangaroo	poult
(e)	sheep	tadpole
(f)	goose	lamb
(g)	hen	kid
(h)	cow	duckling
(i)	frog	cub
(j)	goat	calf
(k)	turkey	joey
(l)	duck	gosling

6. Bird and Animal Similes

A **simile** is a figure of speech in which two things are compared by saying one is 'like' or 'as' the other. Often in a simile, a person is compared to an animal or a bird (e.g. 'Sam Gribley, you had better get down from here *like a rabbit*').

Below is a box of birds and animals.

```
ostrich        lamb
hawk           leech
snake          sheep
eagle          pig
grasshopper    elephant
```

Frightful the Falcon 153

The following sentences contain similes with a blank. Choose the most suitable bird or animal from the box to finish off each of the similes. Use each one only once.

(a) The batsman watched the first delivery like a ....
(b) He clung, like a ...., to the big prop forward's legs.
(c) The crowds, like ...., poured into the store to make their bargain purchases.
(d) Like a ...., the ill-mannered child attacked the plate of stew.
(e) The boxer, looking as jumpy as a ...., moved forward as the bell sounded.
(f) The woman, as gentle as a ...., told the man he had made an error.
(g) Like a striking ...., the thief grabbed the bundle of notes and ran.
(h) He lumbered, like an .... with a load, towards the line.
(i) With eyes like an ...., the young urchin spotted the ring.
(j) Like an .... with head in the sand, she refused to listen.

7. Spelling Search

Each of the following words is taken from the passage, but only every third letter has been provided to help you find the word. Identify each word, and so complete its spelling.

(a) t__ __s__ __d
(b) e__ __r__ __o__
(c) t__ __o__ __
(d) s__ __a__ __l__ __
(e) b__ __l__ __l__ __e
(f) m__ __s__
(g) m__ __v__ __l__ __s
(h) w__ __m__ __
(i) n__ __t__ __n__ __
(j) s__ __a__ __r
(k) b__ __t__ __e__
(l) G__ __b__ __y
(m) a__ __a__ __n__ __y
(n) p__ __f__ __t__ __rs
(o) q__ __v__r

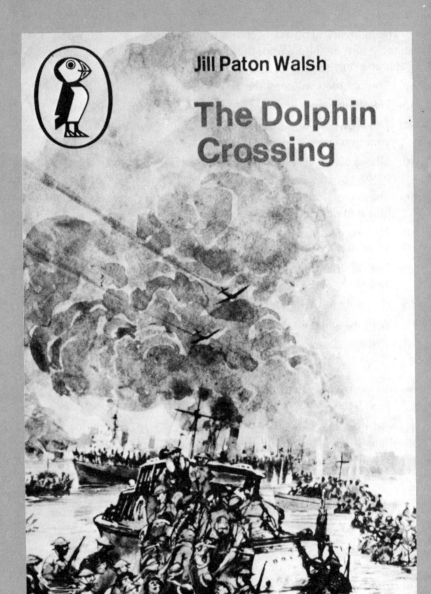

21. The Planes

'The Dolphin Crossing' tells how two boys, Pat and John, take a boat to help rescue some of the soldiers of the British army stranded at Dunkirk.

The planes did not go when they had dropped their bombs. They came back again and again, flying low over the beaches and the shallows, machine-gunning the soldiers and the little boats. A hissing line of bullets spattered the water just in front of *Dolphin's* prow.

John's hands were clenched on the wheel, but his arms were shaking violently from shoulder to wrist. He could hear his teeth chattering, and a hard lump had grown in his stomach, and was pressing against his ribs, so that he had to force himself to breathe. He stood at the wheel, shaking, and *Dolphin* moved steadily in towards the shore. A smoky haze blurred the whole scene. A choking, bitter smell of burning smarted in John's nostrils at every breath. Pat had gone white, and was crouched down against the bench. His pale eyes looked dark; the pupils were widened with fear. John fixed his eyes on a point on the beach ahead, and tried to steer for it, though he could scarcely make his trembling arms move his clenched fists. A lifeboat, full of soldiers, was just being pushed out into the waves ahead of him. He steered to come in beside it.

The planes were coming back again. The noise of their engines as they plunged low over the sands roared in his ears. He looked, and saw one of them coming straight towards *Dolphin*. He flung himself on the cockpit floor, and at the same moment Pat dropped down beside him, and the wave of noise and the sharp cracking of the plane's machine guns went over and past them. They were still alive. They got up.

Where the lifeboat had been there was a blazing wall of flame on the water. Someone was screaming. The flame floated towards them, and sank. John took the wheel, and brought *Dolphin* on course again. She chugged slowly through charred lumps of floating driftwood, until a gentle scrape on *Dolphon's* keel told him she had grounded. The tide was low, and a stretch of shallow water still lay between them and the sand. John put the engine out of gear. The two boys stood and looked round. The water was full of floating bodies. They stained the froth on the waves with faintly visible red streaks. They rolled to and fro in the surf. Some of the soldiers waiting in line on the beach had run forward, and were dragging limp wounded figures from the water.

The hard lump in John's stomach suddenly lurched up his throat. He staggered to the side, doubled up, and vomited into the water.

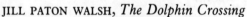
JILL PATON WALSH, *The Dolphin Crossing*

1. Reading for Meaning

(a) Why did the planes fly low over the beaches and the shallows?
(b) How do you know that John was afraid?
(c) Explain why 'a smoky haze blurred the whole scene'.
(d) What was John's plan while the planes were making their first attack?
(e) Why did John fling himself on the cockpit floor?
(f) What happened to the lifeboat with the men in it?
(g) There is a number of words in the passage whose sound conveys the action being described (e.g. 'chugged'). Write down two or three more.
(h) What do we learn about the character of John from this extract?
(i) How does the passage show us that war is horrible?
(j) Explain the meanings of these words.
    (i) prow   (ii) clenched   (iii) charred
    (iv) froth   (v) plunged   (vi) smarted
(You may like to use the back-of-the-book dictionary to help you.)

2. Forming New Words

The words in the left-hand column are taken from *The Planes*. Form new words from these words by filling in the blanks in the words in the right-hand column.

(a)	visible	visib __ l __ ty
(b)	moment	moment __ __ y
(c)	machine	machin __ __ y
(d)	scrape	scrap __ __ __
(e)	noise	nois __
(f)	blazing	blaz __
(g)	violently	violen __ __
(h)	trembling	trembl __
(i)	scene	scene __ __
(j)	scarcely	scarc __ t __

3. Putting the Sentences Back Together

See whether you can put the six disarranged sentences back together again.
(a) did when bombs the go dropped they not their planes had.
(b) the a blurred scene haze whole smoky.
(c) and them flame sank the towards floated.
(d) floating was the bodies of water full.
(e) pushed him waves of into was a full soldiers just of lifeboat being ahead the out.
(f) stood looked two the and boys around.

4. Opposites

These words have been taken from the story. Write down their opposites, (e.g. slowly — quickly).

(a)	gentle	(b)	beside
(c)	forward	(d)	low
(e)	visible	(f)	straight
(g)	dropped	(h)	same
(i)	shallows	(j)	sharp
(k)	full	(l)	alive
(m)	pushed	(n)	floated
(o)	ahead	(p)	over

5. Words that Sound the Same

The following pairs of words sound the same. Most of them are from the story.

past	shore	course	floor
passed	sure	coarse	flaw

Now use them to fill the spaces in the sentences that follow.
(a) John kept the boat on .... as he steered for the ....
(b) There was not a .... in John's plans.
(c) *Dolphin* went .... dead bodies.
(d) John was .... he was doing the right thing.
(e) Pat and John hugged the .... as the planes flew ....
(f) The planes .... over *Dolphin*.
(g) Of ...., there were survivors.
(h) There was a .... feeling to the sand on the shoreline.

6. Changing the Way Sentences are Written

All the sentences are from *The Planes*. Rewrite, using the new beginnings.

(a) A smoky haze blurred the whole scene.
 The whole scene ....
(b) A hard lump had grown in his stomach.
 In his stomach ....
(c) *Dolphin* moved steadily in towards the shore.
 Steadily ....
(d) The flame floated toward them.
 Towards ....
(e) Where the lifeboat had been there was a blazing wall of flame on the water.
 There was a blazing wall ....
(f) John took the wheel and brought *Dolphin* on course again.
 Taking the wheel ....
(g) She chugged slowly through charred lumps of floating driftwood.
 Slowly ....
(h) The planes did not go when they had dropped their bombs.
 Having dropped their bombs, ...

7. Joining Sentences with 'Which' or 'Who'

Join each of the pairs of sentences below using '**who**' or '**which**', e.g.
- The flames floated towards some of the soldiers. The soldiers were screaming in agony.
- The flames floated towards some of the soldiers, **who** were screaming in agony.

(a) The water was full of floating bodies. They stained the froth in the waves with faintly visible red streaks.
(b) John took the wheel. He brought *Dolphin* on course again.
(c) Pat had gone white. He was crouched against the bench.
(d) A hard lump had grown in his stomach. It was pressing against his ribs.
(e) He stood at the wheel of *Dolphin*. *Dolphin* moved steadily in towards the shore.
(f) John fixed his eyes on a point on the beach ahead. John tried to steer for it.

TOPLINER

Sam & Me
Joan Tate

22. Night Terrors

Jo is married to Sam. She desperately wanted a baby and now she has one. There's just one big problem . . .

When I took the baby out for a walk in the afternoon, I had a shock. As I swung the pram round the corner into the park gates, I almost ran into a policeman. He stepped hastily to one side and I stopped with a jerk. Then he smiled at me and said: 'Sorry, madam.' I stood absolutely still and stared in terror. How could he have known I was coming just at that moment? How had he found out? I could feel the sweat trickling down my back and my throat felt quite dry and stiff.

Then he waved his arm and said: 'Carry on,' and my legs walked on. I walked faster and faster and slowly I felt myself coming to life again. How stupid of me. Of course he did not know. I had only imagined that he had looked at me strangely.

After an hour in the park, I went back to my room.

* * *

I had a bad night. I dreamed horrible things and could not remember them when I woke up. And each time I woke up, it was so quiet, I was sure the baby was dead. I kept getting out of bed to see if he was all right, which of course, he was. He was sleeping so soundly, he hardly made a sound.

But I heard all the other sounds. The creak of the bed. The slamming of car doors. The traffic. Someone running down the street. A far distant klaxon wailing its horrible up-and-down wail until it faded away. I lay there willing myself to go to sleep, willing myself not to think about Sam. But it always came back to him. Everything in the end came back to him.

* * *

At three o'clock in the morning I got up and made myself a hot drink. I sat on the edge of that horrible bed, sipping at my drink and trying to think. For the first time I tried to think about the future. Not just tomorrow or the next day. But beyond that.

And that was the first time I really understood what I had done. Up until then I had had so much to think about that was close to me, the baby, his food, somewhere to live, looking after him, where to go, what to do next, that everything else had just vanished to somewhere at the back of my mind.

Now it came to the front. Now in the cold dark hours of the morning in this room, which only yesterday I had felt so secure in, as if I could have stayed in it all day and all night for ever and ever — now it was hostile and the walls seemed to close in on me. I wanted to scream, or cry, or something, but I knew I would wake the baby, so I did not.

I looked at him. For the thousandth time, I just stared at him. He was so small and he needed me. He was the first person ever to need me and this seemed to be so important. But now I saw what I had refused to see before. What I had tucked away, although I knew it to be true, what everyone else knew, what I had blindly, almost madly, ignored.

He wasn't mine.

JOAN TATE, *Sam and Me*

1. Reading for Meaning

(a) What was the shock that Jo had when she took the baby out for a walk?

(b) Jo is not calmed by the policeman's first words to her. What does she do?

(c) 'How had he found out?' Jo asks herself. What is Jo's secret? Read right to the end of the passage to answer this question.

(d) A symptom is a sign — usually of an illness. Jo is suffering from an acute attack of fear. What two bodily symptoms does she become aware of?

(e) Every time she wakes up, the quiet of the room seems to mean one thing to Jo. What is it?

(f) The word 'willing' is used twice. In what two connections?

(g) Her husband, Sam, means a lot to Jo. How do we know this?

(h) Give six practical reasons why Jo, at first, is unable to think about the future.

(i) The room has changed from being one thing to being another. Be more exact.

(j) Why does the baby seem so important to Jo?

2. Spelling Words

absolutely	secure
hastily	hostile
imagined	tomorrow
strangely	thousandth
remember	important

Now select the right word to fit each clue.
(a) Find the word that ends with something you'd put on a roof.
(b) Find the word that ends with something that beats a disease.
(c) Find the word that contains a medieval musical instrument.
(d) Find the word that includes a heavenly being.
(e) Find a word that begins with the present tense of 'had'.
(f) Find the word that contains something gritty.
(g) Find a word that ends with an argument.
(h) Find the word that contains the word that is opposite to 'starboard'.
(i) Find the word that contains 3 e's in this pattern: __e__e__ __e__.
(j) Find the word that is made up of exactly 4 vowels and 4 consonants.

3. Wanted: Words that Fit

Here's a summary of the story *Sam and Me*, from which the passage is taken. See if you can place the WANTED words as you rewrite the summary in your workbook.

Sam and Me

'Sam and Me' is the .... of Jo, a girl who came from a .... home to live in a .... family. It's the story of how she .... up and how she got to know Sam.

Why did Jo end up in a .... room alone with a baby?

An .... can be a .... as this .... story shows. It's a story about the real .... in ....

WANTED WORDS		
absorbing	beginning	life
	real	
things	grew	children's
	furnished	end
	story	

4. Adjective – Noun Link-Up

Adjectives add to the meaning of **nouns**. In the passage, there are plenty of things that are carefully described.

The nouns in the box and the adjectives below go together in the passage. Link them up. There are two nouns that have two adjectives linked with them.

NOUNS	
gates	time
doors	klaxon
night	person
things	bed
drink	day
hours	sounds

ADJECTIVES

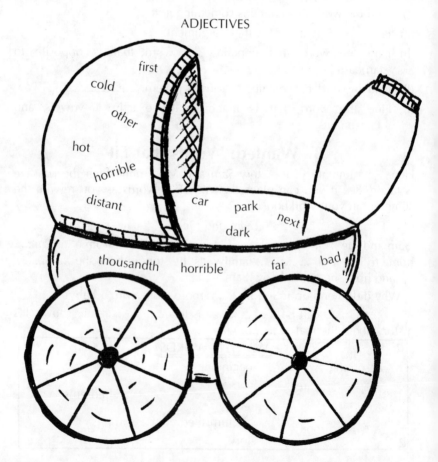

first, cold, other, hot, horrible, distant, car, park, dark, next, thousandth, horrible, far, bad

5. Homonyms

Homonyms are words that **sound** alike but are **spelt** differently.

For each word from the passage, find another word that sounds the same but is spelt differently and that will fit the circles. Write your answers in your workbook.

○
h e a r d
○
○

Clue: Cattle form this

○
○○ n
e

Clue: Came first

c ○○○○○
o
u
r
s
e

Clue: Rough

c
r
○○ e ○○
a
k

Clue: A small waterway

s a w
○
○
○

Clue: Painful

q ○○○○
u
i
t
e

Clue: Completely

s
u
r
○○○○ e

Clue: Where the waves end

○
s e e
○

Clue: Vast, salty

○
○
○
w a i l
○

Clue: A great and intelligent creature of the deep

○
n o t
○
○

Clue: A twist in rope

6. Word Families

Rewrite the following sentences, filling in the blank spaces as you go. Choose words that will suit the sense of the sentences from the brackets of words 'families'.

(a) I walked faster and faster and .... I felt myself coming to life again. [slow, slowly, slowness]

(b) I had only .... that he had looked at me .... [strangeness, strange, strangely; imagine, imaginatively, imagined, imagination]

(c) And each time I .... up, it was so ...., I was sure the baby was dead. [quiet, quietly; wake, woke, woken]

(d) I sat on the edge of that horrible bed, sipping at my drink and .... to .... [try, tried, trying; thought, think, thoughtfully, thoughtful]

(e) And that was the first time I really .... what I had .... [understood, understand, understanding, understandingly; did, do, done]

(f) He was so small and he .... me. [need, needful, needed, needy]

(g) But now I saw what I had .... to .... before. [saw, seen, see; refuse, refusing, refused, refusal]

(h) He was .... so soundly, he hardly .... a sound. [slept, sleep, sleeper, sleeping; made, makes, making]

7. Pronouns? No Problems!

Joan Tate naturally prefers to use pronouns instead of repeating 'Jo' or 'Sam' or 'the policeman' or 'the baby'. However, three rules need to be kept in mind when using pronouns:

- When a pronoun is the subject of a verb, the nominative case of the pronoun is used:

    He (not *him*) smiled at me

- When a pronoun follows a preposition, the pronoun has to be in the objective case:

    He smiled at *me* (not *I*)

- When a pronoun is the object of a verb, the objective case of the pronoun is used:

    He kept *me* (not *I*) busy.

Here's a useful guide to the case of pronouns:

NOMINATIVE	OBJECTIVE
I you he she it we you they	me you him her it us you them

Keeping the rules in mind, and checking with the table, rewrite the following sentences putting in the pronoun of your choice from the brackets.

(a) How stupid of .... [I/me]

(b) .... had only imagined that .... had looked at .... strangely. [me/I, he/him, me/I]

(c) Up till then .... had had so much to think about that was close to .... [me/I, I/me]

(d) Now in the cold dark hours of the morning in this room, which only yesterday .... had felt so secure in, as if .... could have stayed in it all day and all night for ever and ever — now it was hostile and the walls seemed to close in on .... [me/I, I/me, me/I]

(e) He was the first person ever to need .... [I/me]

(f) It was going to be a hard time for .... [them/they]

(g) It's best for .... if .... live alone. [we/us, we/us]

(h) For the thousandth time .... just stared at .... [me/I, him/he]

(i) .... managed to look after both of .... though it was hard for .... [she/her, they/them, her/she]

23. Saved

Gilly Ground is eleven years old. After getting thrown out of an orphanage, he is taken to live with Kobalt, the carpenter. Kobalt is mentally unbalanced and when Gilly escapes Kobalt tries to kill him.

I get to my feet and look from the slit of a window. The squat, invincible hulk that is Kobalt is waving its arms wildly. The sack of food flies into the air from his left hand like the body of a small animal and smashes against the trunk of a tree. And in his right is the uplifted shape of an iron-headed hammer as large as an axe.

'Come out! I order you out!' he shouts. 'If I can't have you the way I want you I'll have you dead!'

It is now. I know it is now. I can stand still in my nothingness and be murdered or I can fight for my life. I am suddenly free, free of the orphanage, the bondage of Kobalt, free even of myself. I don't decide. I don't even think. I move.

I pick up a handful of stones and shower them at the enemy. One of them gets his shoulder. He grunts and halts his advance. 'That will do you no good!' he yells, though he is so near I would hear him whisper. 'I will have you under the earth sooner or later!'

I use these seconds to rearm. The next hail of rocks I aim higher and two small ones bounce off his forehead.

He raises his hammer to the sky, whirling it like a sling. If I can de-weapon him I've got a better chance, not much but better. 'Throw it!' I call out. 'Go on get me!' I step into the entrance of the tower in full view.

The man tilts his massive head backwards and booms into hideous laughter. 'I'm not that stupid, my little cock! Crow on! I'll snap you off at the neck by sun-up!'

He blocks me like an oak, so solid, so strong he might be rooted. I realize my sole hope is to get past him somehow, dodge the slaughtering swipe of that deadly hammer, and, because I can't run, roll down the mountain to get a head start on his pursuit. I have to show myself, come all the way into the open. I know it may be a fool's move but it is the only one I have. The tower has become a trap.

I feel one stroke of the rising sun like a last blessing on my cheeks as I come forward — a final touch of life. A blur of wood and iron swishes past my left ear as I duck and try to swerve out of range. I stumble and go down on my knees.

'I've got you now!' screeches the madman. He lunges in for the kill.

I hug my arms around me tight like I used to my grandmother when the dark had almost conquered me. I wait for death.

But suddenly I am still here and Kobalt is enwrapped in a fury of snarls and snaps and mud-coloured fur! Blood streaks the man's neck and something as savage as a bullwhip is tearing at his right arm. The hammer careens down the hill and Kobalt is thrashing in all directions trying to throw off this ferocious hound of hell. It is Mash!

The man leaps backwards, trips, and crashes onto his spine. The dog covers him from knee to neck, teeth bared and about to clench into his flesh. But Kobalt is still, as still as the boulder under his head.

I throw myself onto the dog and pull him off. I hang on until the shudders leave his bony frame and his heaving breath quiets to quick panting. I loosen my hold and he turns his eyes to mine and licks my face.

'That's enough,' I sort of croon in his lank ear. 'He is alive. Leave him that way. It's better for both of us.'

Mash tells me he understands and consents with his now truly wagging tail.

JULIA CUNNINGHAM, Dorp Dead

1. Reading for Meaning

(a) 'Invincible' means 'not able to be defeated'. Why does 'invincible' seem appropriate to describe Kobalt?

(b) 'He blocks me like an oak'. What does 'like an oak' tell us about Kobalt? What word in the same line carries on this comparison?

(c) Why does the boy decide to show himself?

(d) Do you think the boy expected to be killed? Why?

(e) How do you know that the dog, Mash, loved the boy?
(f) Do you think Mash would have killed Kobalt? Explain your view.
(g) What comments would you make about the character of the boy?
(h) What comments would you make about the character of Kobalt?
(i) What does the boy mean when he says, 'Leave him that way. It's better for both of us'?
(j) What is the meaning of the following words?

  (i) bared (ii) lank
  (iii) careens (iv) de-weapon

(You may like to use the back-of-the-book dictionary.)

2. Complete the Following Table

Some of the endings have been given to help you.

	NOUN	VERB	ADJECTIVE
(a)	__ion	decide	__ve
(b)		murder	__ous
(c)			pursuing
(d)		__en	strong
(e)		__en	deadly
(f)	fury	__iate	
(g)	__ity	__fy	stupid
(h)		__ize	final
(i)	__ss	loosen	

3. Unscramble the Sound Words

Below are mixed-up words that indicate the sounds made by Kobalt, the boy, and Mash, the dog (l e y s l = yells). Find the sound words.

(a) n o r o c
(b) s u n r t g
(c) h e p s i r w
(d) s s t u o h
(e) s e s e c c e r h
(f) l a c l
(g) h a g t u l r e
(h) s m o o b
(i) s s l a r n

4. Finding New Words

Rewrite the sentences replacing the writer's words that are in bold (or heavy) type with words of your own that have similar meanings.

(a) I **get to my feet** and look from the **slit** of the window.
(b) 'Come out! I **order** you out!' he **shouts**.
(c) I can stand still in my nothingness and be **murdered** or I can **fight** for my **life**.
(d) The man tilts his **massive** head backwards and booms into **hideous** laughter.
(e) I **realize** my **sole** hope is to get past him somehow, **dodge** the **slaughtering** swipe of that deadly hammer.
(f) I **stumble** and go down on my knees.
(g) He **raises** his hammer **to the sky, whirling** it like a sling.
(h) I **know** it may be a **fool's** move, but it is the **only** one I have.

5. Spelling

invincible	massive	ferocious
murdered	hideous	directions
orphanage	slaughtering	conquered
bondage	pursuit	loosen
shoulder	screeches	enough

6. The Comparison of Adjectives

Complete the following table. The first two have been done for you.

	POSITIVE	COMPARATIVE	SUPERLATIVE
	tall	taller	tallest
	famous	more famous	most famous
(a)	sad		
(b)	strong		
(c)	good		
(d)	bad		
(e)	deadly		
(f)	large		
(g)	furious		

7. Find-A-Word

Using the clues below, find the words in the spelling list opposite.
(a) This word is the opposite of 'freedom'.
(b) A place where children are kept.
(c) The opposite of 'tighten'.
(d) This word means 'defeated'.
(e) This word means 'very big'.
(f) This word is 'very fierce'.
(g) This word is connected with 'homicide'.
(h) This destructive word has a bit of fun in it.
(i) This word ends with something businessmen wear.
(j) This word rhymes with 'peaches'.

24. Disaster on the Lawn

Hortense, a four-year-old deer complete with antlers, is Gerald Durrell's first large pet. He takes Hortense for a walk across the golf-links and everything goes well; yet Gerald is worried about his family's reaction to Hortense.

I was not popular that week. My marmoset had tried to climb into bed with Larry in the early morning and, on being repulsed, had bitten him in the ear; my magpies had uprooted a whole row of tomatoes carefully planted by my other brother, Leslie; and one of my grass snakes had escaped and been found with piercing screams by my sister Margo behind the sofa cushions. I was determined, therefore, that Hortense should be kept well away from the family. However, my hopes were short-lived.

It was one of those rare days you sometimes get in an English summer when the sun actually shines, and Mother, carried away by this phenomenon, had decided to have tea on the lawn. So when Hortense and I got back from our walk across the golf-links we were treated to the sight of the family sitting in deck-chairs grouped round a trolley on which reposed the accoutrements of tea-making, sandwiches, a plum cake, and large bowls of raspberries and cream. Coming suddenly round the side of the house and finding my family thus arrayed took me aback. Not so Hortense, who with one glance took in the peaceful scene. He decided that between him and the safety of the garage lay a monstrous and probably dangerous enemy with four wheels — a tea trolley. There was only one thing he could do. Uttering a harsh bleat as war cry, he lowered his head and charged, whipping his lead out of my fingers. He hit the trolley amidships, getting his horns tangled and showering tea things in all directions.

My family were completely trapped, for it is extraordinarily difficult, if not impossible, to leave a deck-chair with alacrity even in moments of crisis. The result was that Mother was scalded with boiling tea, my sister was bespattered with cucumber sandwiches and Larry and Leslie received, in equal quantities, the raspberries and cream.

'It's the last straw!' roared Larry, flicking mashed raspberries from his trousers. 'Get that bloody animal out of here, do you hear?'

'Now, now, dear! Language,' said Mother pacifically. 'It was an accident. The poor animal didn't mean it.'

'Didn't mean it? Didn't mean it?' said Larry, his face suffused.

He pointed a quivering finger at Hortense, who, somewhat alarmed by the havoc he had created, was standing there demurely with the tea cloth hitched to his antlers, like a wedding veil.

'You saw it deliberately charge the trolley, and you say it didn't mean it?'

'What I mean, dear,' said Mother, flustered, 'is that it didn't mean to put the raspberries on you.'

'I don't care what it meant,' said Larry vehemently. 'I don't want to know what it meant. All I know is that Gerry must get rid of it. I will not have rampaging brutes like that around. Next time it might be one of us it attacks. Who the hell do you think I am? Buffalo Bill Cody?'

So, in spite of my pleas, Hortense was banished to a nearby farm, and with his departure vanished my only chance of experience with large animals in the home. It seemed there was only one thing for me to do — get a job in a zoo.

GERALD DURRELL, *Beasts in My Belfry*

1. Reading for Meaning

(a) Larry, Leslie and Margo are members of the Durrell family. Link each of them with a pet of Gerald's and, briefly, say why each of them ended up disliking the pet.

(b) Why did Gerald's mother decide to have tea on the lawn?

(c) What word describes the scene that Gerald and Hortense see as they round the corner of the house?

(d) Why does the tea trolley pose a threat to Hortense?

(e) When Hortense hit the trolley, Gerald's family were showered with tea things. Why were they unable to avoid them?

(f) Who is most upset and what words recall previous bad experiences?

(g) Who, rather unexpectedly, comes to the defence of Hortense?

(h) What particular words lead to an argument?

(i) There is something about Hortense that recalls a ceremony. What is it and what is the ceremony?

(j) As a result of his experience with Hortense, Gerald Durell narrows down his choice of a future career. What is it likely to be?

2. Spelling

Here are spelling words from *Disaster on the Lawn*.

repulsed	extraordinarily	havoc
phenomenon	alacrity	demurely
accoutrements	crisis	vehemently
reposed	bespattered	rampaging
arrayed	pacifically	banished
monstrous	suffused	

(a) Some **a**'s are placed below. Find the spelling·words they belong to and write them in your workbook.

```
_ _ _ _ a _ _ _ _ _ _
         _ a _ _ _ _
      a _ _ _ _ _ _ _ _ _ _ _
       _ a _ _ _ _ _ _
        a _ _ a _ _ _ _
       a _ a _ _ _ _ _ _
         _ _ _ _ a _ _ _ _ _ a _ _ _ _
```

(b) Given the word 'crisis', fit 8 words from the spelling list into the crossword. Here's a clue. None of them contains an 'a'.

3. Dictionary

Look up the meaning of each of these words from *Disaster on the Lawn* in the back-of-the-book dictionary. Then use each of them where it will fit and make sense in the sentences below.

(a) When Larry was told that Hortense did did not mean to spill the raspberries on him he answered ....

(b) Many luxury items ready for tea .... on the trolley.

(c) It is impossible to get up from a deck-chair with any .... even in a ....

(d) Hortense had created .... when he charged the trolley and bowled it over.

(e) One of Gerald's pets had paid Larry back for being .... by biting him.

(f) Unfortunately for Gerald, the problem of Hortense was solved when he was .... to a farm.

(g) All the things on the trolley that are going to be used for tea-making are called its ....

(h) After the battle with the trolley, Hortense tries to escape judgement by standing very ....

(i) Obviously a rare day of sun in an English summer is fit to be called a ....

(j) If something is extremely hard to do it can be said to be .... difficult.

(k) Mother tries to keep the peace between Larry and Gerald by speaking ....

(l) Gerald saw the members of his family .... or spread out comfortably in deck-chairs on the lawn.

(m) Margo did not get around to eating a single sandwich although she was .... with plenty of them.

(n) Larry was so angry, his face became ....

(o) '................' was the word used by Larry to describe the way Hortense went on his attacking and destroying spree.

(p) Hortense decided that the trolley was a .... foe.

4. Painless Punctuation

First let's have a quick run through the most common punctuation marks. Sentences begin with a capital letter and end with either a full stop (.) for a statement, an exclamation mark (!) for an exclamation or a question mark (?) for a question.

Capital letters are also used to begin the names of people and of relatives when they stand for a particular person and are used as a name. And, of course, use a capital for 'I'.

Quotation marks (single or double — they are single in the passage) are used to enclose actual speech, and any other punctuation marks (. ! ?) that occur in actual speech.

Commas are used where a natural pause occurs in a sentence.

Rewrite the following sentences, putting in the punctuation marks needed as you go.

(a) who the hell do you thing i am buffalo bill cody

(b) the result was that mother was scalded with boiling tea my sister was bespattered with cucumber sandwiches and larry and leslie received in equal quantities the raspberries and cream

(c) you saw it deliberately charge the trolley and you say it didn't mean it

(d) i don't care what it meant said larry vehemently

(e) didn't mean it didn't mean it said larry his face suffused

(f) it's the last straw roared larry flicking mashed raspberries from his trousers

(g) now now dear language said mother pacifically

(h) what i mean dear said mother flustered is that it didn't mean to put the raspberries on you

Finished? Check back with the passage!

5. Clinging Couples

Link up the words in the left-hand column that often go with words from the right-hand column. They are all from the passage, and several of them cling so tightly they even have hyphens (-).

golf-	screams
early	trolley
plum	straw
war	chair
tea	veil
deck-	making
last	morning
wedding	cry
tea-	lived
piercing	cake
short-	links

6. Drop-Outs

Drop out letters from passage words and arrive at new words. The first letter is given in brackets.

(a) Drop 4 letters from *marmoset* to arrive at the red planet.   Mars

(b) Drop 4 letters from *escaped* to be feeling unhappy.   [s]

(c) Drop 3 letters from *tangled* to get a story.   [t]

(d) Drop 8 letters from *accoutrements* for a fast, heavenly body.   [c]

(e) Drop 9 letters from *extraordinary* to hear a loud, animal noise.   [r]

(f) Drop 6 letters from *impossible* and find a heap.   [p]

(g) Drop 5 letters from *sometimes* and do a silent act-out.   [m]

(h) Drop 5 letters from *bespattered* for some floury mixture (also 'to hit').   [b]

(i) Drop 3 letters from *reposed* and pick a flower.   [r]

(j) Drop
    (i) 4 letters from *deliberately* to get a verb meaning 'to free'.   [l]
    (ii) 8 letters from *deliberately* to get a word meaning 'not on time'.   [l]

(k) Drop
    (i)   4 letters from *planted* and out crawls a small insect.   [a]
    (ii) 3 letters from *planted* for a short street.   [l]
    (iii) 3 letters from *planted* for some heavy breathing.   [p]

(l) Drop
    (i)   6 letters from *determined* for eating in style.   [d]
    (ii) 6 letters from *determined* for part of a school year.   [t]
    (iii) 6 letters from *determined* for a place where minerals come from.   [m]

7. Stay Agreeable

Verbs and subjects have to agree. Here are the rules!
- A singular subject takes a singular verb.
- A plural subject takes a plural verb.

His **hope was** short-lived. [singular subject, singular verb]

His **hopes were** short-lived. [plural subject, plural verb]

Rewrite the following sentences, making the words in bold (or heavy) type either singular or plural. You may also need to change the rest of the sentence slightly.

(a) The **tomato belongs** to Leslie.

(b) My **marmoset has** tried to climb into bed with Larry.

(c) Gerald's **story is** all about his pets.

(d) There **is** no **fly** on Hortense.

(e) **Deck-chairs are** placed on the lawn.

(f) A **deer** often **does** the unexpected.

(g) Tea-making luxury **items stand** on the trolley.

(h) Gerald's **pet shows** that an **animal has** a **mind** of **its** own.

(i) An **animal knows** how to look innocent.

(j) The big **animal goes** for **its** enemy, the tea-trolley.

8. Vocabulary Add-In

Here's a summary of the book *Beasts in My Belfry* from which the passage is taken. From the panel, fill in the missing words by rewriting, in your workbook, the phrases or sentences in which the missing words are located. Words marked * are in the back-of-the-book dictionary.

Beasts in My Belfry

Gerald Durrell was .... in India but .... with his family to England when he was three. Five years later they went to live on the Continent, and .... settled on the island of Corfu.

From the age of two, Gerald had been .... by .... and soon had a large .... of local animals as pets. But as his unofficial zoo grew, so did his family's .... The only .... was to find another, more .... zoo.

So in 1945 he joined Whipsnade as a .... keeper with Albert the lion, Babs the polar bear and a baby Père David deer among his first charges. In this .... entertaining history, Gerald Durrell .... all the fun of those early years.

The book is full of larger-than-life animal ...., among them Teddy the Bear, who sang operatic arias with one paw clasped to his breast, Peter the Giraffe and his bosom friend Billy the Goat, dancing gnus, playful zebras and a .... of others.

characters	returned
host*	hilariously*
recaptures	fascinated
hostility*	permanent
collection	zoology*
born	eventually*
student	solution*

The Men from
P.I.G. & R.O.B.O.T.

Harry Harrison

25. The Wild Ones

Ever dreamed of being helped in everything you do by a master computer which controls a team of robots from tiny spider size to ones which carry atomic weapons? Meet someone who's got it all already — Henry Venn, Space Patrolman with R.O.B.O.T.

They proceeded in silence then, climbing through the knee-high grass and pushing under the lowhanging fronds of the trees. The spider silently led the way on to an outcropping of rock and pointed below. Henry took off his hat and laid it on the ground before crawling forward to look carefully over the edge. It was quite a sight.

What appeared to be a well charred and half eaten side of beef lay in a cold bed of ashes just below him. Next to it, half on the grass and half in the ashes, sprawled a singularly unattractive member of the human race. His clothes, if they could be called that, consisted of a collection of badly tanned furs laced together with rough strips of leather. Long knotted hair merged into an even longer and more tangled beard. Hair, furs and man were matted and filthy and now liberally strewn with ashes. The furs had fallen back to disclose the individual's monstrously engorged stomach that rose up like an over-ripe melon; he had obviously stuffed himself to partial extinction on the feast of burnt meat. Something troubled him now, undoubtedly his digestion, and he groaned and rolled without opening his eyes. His hand, which rested in the ashes, crawled over like an immense insect and plucked at the beef until it detached a fragment. This was conveyed to the gaping mouth and chewed and swallowed apparently without the feaster waking up.

'Very nice,' Henry said, standing and brushing himself off and putting the derby back on his head. 'There goes my appetite for the week. Let's see what Rosebud has to say for himself?' The spider jumped to his shoulder as he slid down the slope to the dell below.

The Wild One was awake instantly, sitting up — which took quite an effort — and glaring at Henry from a pair of very piggy and bloodshot eyes.

'Very pleased to meet you, sir, and happy to see that you have dined well. Let me introduce myself . . .'

'Kill! Kill!' the Wild One grunted and took up the stone hammer that he had been lying on, hurling it at Henry in a single, surprisingly swift motion. Straight at his forehead. There was no time to dodge or to even raise his arm in defence.

The robot spider hurled itself from his shoulder, making eight nice little holes in his skin with its feet as it did so, and crashed into the hammer. Hammer and spider fell to the ground in a tangle of metal legs, the spider crushed and unmoving.

'I assure you, sir, that I mean you no harm . . .'

'Kill! Kill!' the Wild One mumbled again, feeling about for a fist-sized rock that he hurled as well. Prepared this time, Henry dodged the missile.

'Come now, we can discuss this like grown men . . .'

'Kill! Kill!' the Wild One screeched and rushed to the attack, fingers spread. Henry stepped inside the clawing arms and administered a swift chop with the side of his hand to the other's neck. Then stepped aside as the attacker went down and out.

'I am afraid that you and I have a problem in communication,' he said as he bent to wipe the greasy side of his hand on the grass. An insect buzzed about his head and he swatted at it before he heard the reedy voice it whispered with.

'Report. Another Wild One is coming this way up the ravine. He does not appear to be armed.'

'A small blessing,' Henry said, settling himself into a fighting stance, extended hands ready.

HARRY HARRISON, *The Men From P.I.G. and R.O.B.O.T.*

1. Reading for Meaning

(a) What really was the insect that buzzed around Henry's head?
(b) Explain why Henry took off his hat before crawling forward.
(c) Why was the speed with which the Wild One threw his axe at Henry 'surprisingly swift'?
(d) Who said 'I assure you, sir, that I mean you no harm . . .'?
(e) What is meant by 'the attacker went down and out'?
(f) Account for the fact that Henry's hand was 'greasy' after hitting the Wild One.
(g) What was strange about the way the Wild One ate as Henry watched from cover?
(h) How was the Wild One clothed?
(i) How many feet did the robot spider have?
(j) Why did Henry feel he'd lose his appetite for a week?
(k) Why had Henry not seen the Wild One's stone hammer?

2. Character Description

Below is a list of words and phrases which suitably describe either Henry or the Wild One. Draw up two columns in your work book, one for Henry and one for the Wild One, and separate out the words which fit each one.

unruffled	violent
composed	polite
dull-witted	calm
nervous	illiterate
competent	cautious
a skilled fighter	dirty
ill-mannered	gluttonous
educated	possessing a sense of humour
overweight	inarticulate
filthy	

HENRY	WILD ONE
polite	dirty

3. Understatement

Understatement is the opposite of exaggeration. Instead of describing something and exaggerating, or even describing it just as it is or happened, in understatement we deliberately play it down and describe it as less sensational. Understatement is usually humorous in its effect.

Henry is confronted by an unbelievably filthy, ugly, wild, insane person who makes three attempts to kill him in a matter of a few seconds and is finally knocked out by a judo chop from Henry.

Henry's comment? A beautiful example of understatement! 'I am afraid that you and I have a problem in communication.'

Try your hand at making up an understatement that you can imagine coming from the lips of Henry following each of the following situations.

(a) A vehicle roars out to where Henry has parked his space-ship and, just as Henry is about to welcome him, the rider pulls out a gun and tries to shoot Henry. Fortunately the attempt fails, and the rider roars off again.

(b) Henry's ship-computer has used robots to drill a tunnel for Henry, which unfortunately caves in and almost traps our hero when he climbs through it.

(c) With Henry safe in his spaceship, a large mob of men roars into view. They proceed to fire at his ship with all the weapons at their disposal. Only when they see they aren't getting anywhere do they race away on their machines.

(d) Henry is riding his gyroscopic unicycle into the nearby city when he is confronted by a woman and two children. They plead for his help in getting away from their planet.

(e) Henry has asked the computer to keep things under control while he pays a visit to one of the nearby houses to gather more information. When he comes out he is confronted by a truck charging at him out of the darkness, and guns blazing at him.

(f) Henry has asked his computer to get him 'a sleeping bag or something' ready so he can sleep in the nearby hills. When he arrives he finds a neat tent staked out with flags flying, a brass bedstead, a table and easy chair and a magnificent meal to eat by candlelight.

4. Comparatives and Superlatives

In the extract we are told that the Wild One's hair was 'long' but his beard was 'longer'. His hair is 'knotted' and tangled and his beard 'more tangled'.

When two things are compared we use what is called the **comparative** degree of an adjective. This is formed by adding '**-er**' to the adjective in some cases or placing '**more**' in front in other cases. When three or more things are compared we use what is called the **superlative** degree of the adjective. This is formed by adding '**-est**' to the adjective in some cases or in other cases putting '**most**' in front of it.

Complete the following table of **comparatives** and **superlatives**. All adjectives are from the passage. The first two have been done for you.

	ADJECTIVE	COMPARATIVE	SUPERLATIVE
	long	longer	longest
	tangled	more tangled	most tangled
(a)	cold		
(b)	immense		
(c)	nice		
(d)	happy		
(e)	swift		
(f)	little		
(g)	straight		
(h)	greasy		
(i)	needy		
(j)	small		

5. R.O.B.O.T. Crossword

Across

3 What the spider's legs were made of
4 Leather ...... were used to lace the Wild One's furs together
5 Liberally strewn on the Wild One
7 The Wild One's way of looking at Henry through his piggy eyes
9 How Henry approached the edge to look over into the Wild One's camp

Down

1 The Wild One had been feasting on burnt ...
2 The new Wild One was approaching along this
4 Something the Wild One seemed able to do without waking
6 How the spider moved itself to intercept the hammer
8 Where Henry wiped his greasy fingers

6. Words and Meanings

Find words in the extract with the following meanings. The first letter of each word is given to help you.

(a) Burnt on the outside   c_ _ _ _ _ _
(b) An object which is fired or thrown   m_ _ _ _ _ _
(c) A movement   m_ _ _ _ _
(d) A small part of something   f_ _ _ _ _ _ _
(e) Scattered around   s_ _ _ _ _
(f) Not pleasant to look at   u_ _ _ _ _ _ _ _ _ _ _
(g) Over-filled   e_ _ _ _ _ _ _
(h) Carried   c_ _ _ _ _ _ _
(i) To reveal   d_ _ _ _ _ _ _
(j) Disconnected, removed   d_ _ _ _ _ _ _
(k) Tangled and knotted   m_ _ _ _ _
(l) A particular body posture adopted while standing   s_ _ _ _ _

7. Punctuation

Correctly punctuate the following.

I am ready henry said pressing the dispose button on the coffee cup and throwing it over the cliff it disintegrated into a cloud of fine dust before it had dropped ten feet how do we contact our subject the skyhook will take you as close as possible without your being observed the robot spider said riding the ladder that swung close to henry he grabbed a rung I will guide you the rest of the way

26. A Viking Raid

Captured after stealing fabulous weapons, including the horned helmet, from the burial mound of a dead king, the three Vikings — Starkad, Gauk and Beorn — are sentenced by the headman of the village they raided.

At last the headman said, 'Look you, sailormen, what I have to do, I have to do, and there is no getting away from it. The doom was passed on you by my Council while you were still asleep. If I let you go, they would turn on me and say I was no true leader. Then I should feel the axe-kiss; and I have a wife and family to care for. I did not come all the way from Roeskilde to have my head set on a pole, I can tell you. But I will do what I can — I will have a good breakfast set before you, so that you will make the journey to Valhalla on a full stomach.'

Starkad shook his head and said, 'Do not put the cook to the trouble, friend. We have caused you enough work as it is, and to waste good food would be a crime.'

The headman smiled and nodded to the axe-man, who took out a whetstone and started to put a good edge on the blade. While he was doing this, Gauk ignored him and said to Starkad, 'Friend, every day brings us something to learn. For years I have wondered how it feels to be dead, now I am going to find out — and that without any trouble to myself. That is the wonderful thing about it!'

Starkad said thoughtfully, 'I have wondered, as well. What puzzles me is — when the head is off, and lying on the ground, can it still think?'

Gauk scratched his own shaggy head at this, then said, 'Look, baresark, I have an idea; you see this cloakpin in my hand? Well, after the axe-man has done his work, I will stick this pin into the oak-log if I still know anything. Will that answer your question?'

Starkad nodded and said, 'Aye, well enough, comrade. At least, if worst comes to worst, Beorn and I will know the answer, though you may not.'

Gauk smiled and said, 'Very well, so be it. I am ready with the pin. Strike now, axe-man!'

Beorn shut his eyes when the axe came down. He heard the thud and hated to look, though he was as anxious as Starkad to see what Gauk did with the cloak-pin.

But he did nothing; it lay, glimmering in the morning sun, beside the log. Starkad said, 'Well, that is another riddle answered, lad.'

Then he smiled, and turned his head towards the axe-man. 'Be about it,' he said. 'I've got a cramp starting in my right leg.'

Beorn covered his face with his hands, but before he did this, Starkad nodded to him and winked as merrily as if they shared a great joke. He heard the viking say softly, 'Wait on, Gauk! I'm almost with you now, friend.'

Then all at once, the air was pierced through with loud cries and the furious buzzing of arrows. Beorn heard one thump into the log beside him, and then a deep groan. He opened his eyes again and saw the axe-man on his knees beside Gauk, fumbling at a shaft which was in his arm.

Dust rose everywhere. Feet banged on the ground. Sarkad smiled and leaned over to the axe-man. 'Lend me your knife,' he said pleasantly, then cut the cords which bound his ankles.

He stood up and stretched, then flung the knife back in the wounded man, who was beyond caring whether his property was returned or not.

'Come, Beorn,' said Starkad, 'I'll take Gauk's helmet and don't you forget your sword.' Bending, he snatched up the horned helmet and longsword, and, taking Beorn by the belt, swung him on to his feet.

All happened so fast that the lad hardly knew where he was, or what had taken place.

Then, from behind the headman's thatched hut, he heard Jarl Skallagrim's voice yelling, 'Run, run! The tide is on the turn, we cannot wait for ever!'

Villagers lay tumbled beside huts and against rocks, caught by this deadly raid.

HENRY TREECE, *Horned Helmet*

A Viking Raid   195

1. Reading for Meaning

(a) What three reasons does the headman give for not being able to free his captives?
(b) The headman promises to do what he can for the captives — but what does this amount to?
(c) How does Starkad make a joke about his own coming death?
(d) What is Gauk soon going to find out more about?
(e) Starkad is puzzled by something gruesome. What is it? (Use the back-of-the-book dictionary.)
(f) 'Well, that is another riddle answered, lad.' Outline the riddle and say how it is answered.
(g) How does Starkad show his courage (with a touch of humour) in the face of his own death?
(h) What happenings suddenly herald the arrival of rescuers?
(i) 'Lend me your knife.' Why is the axe-man unable to refuse Starkad's request?
(j) What kind of rescue is suggested by the information yelled by Jarl Skallagrim?

2. Spelling

journey	furious
stomach	groan
ignored	pleasantly
thoughtfully	property
answer	happened
question	merrily
anxious	

(a) Draw up the 'spaces and symbols' grid into your workbook.
(b) Fill in seven words from the spellings box using the clues.
(c) Find an extra 4 list words by taking the letters in
   (i) the squares
   (ii) the circles
   (iii) the triangles
   (iv) the diamonds
   and rearranging them to form words.
(d) Clues and symbols give you 11 words. Fit the two left-over words in the list into these spaces: _ _ _ _ _ _ _ _   _ _ _ _ _ _ _ _

SPACES AND SYMBOLS

Clues
(1) Something you own
(2) Enjoyably
(3) This can suffer a pain
(4) A reply
(5) With a little mental effort
(6) Something to ask
(7) Not given any attention

3. Pinning Down the Opposites

Each of the passage words on the left has an antonym or opposite somewhere on the right. Find the elusive antonym and write down both passage word and antonym in your workbook. Note: some antonyms can be formed simply by adding 'un' to the front of the word.

	PASSAGE WORDS	ANTONYMS
(a)	question	husband
(b)	true	play
(c)	forget	bad
(d)	asleep	answer
(e)	caught	best
(f)	leader	left
(g)	wife	false
(h)	work	awake
(i)	good	uncovered
(j)	smiled	remember
(k)	dead	unready
(l)	worst	follower
(m)	ready	loudly
(n)	shut	frowned
(o)	right	freed
(p)	covered	alive
(q)	softly	open

4. Sound Off

Some words resemble actual sounds, e.g. the **clash** of swords. Hear the sound of metal on metal?

There are some sound words in *A Viking Raid*. In the same way that 'clash' goes with 'swords', the sounds of the words on the arrows go with the target words. Link them up.

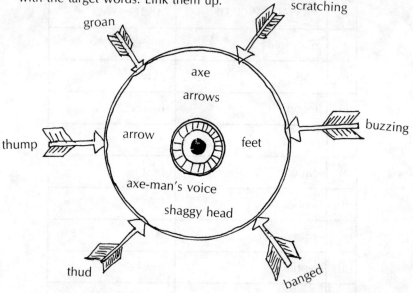

Here are some more common sound words. Link them up with their appropriate nouns.

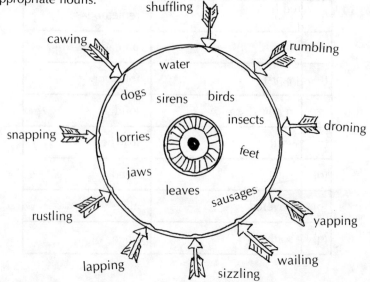

A Viking Raid 199

5. Axed Sentences

Sentences from the passage have been axed at critical points. By checking back with the passage, rejoin them.

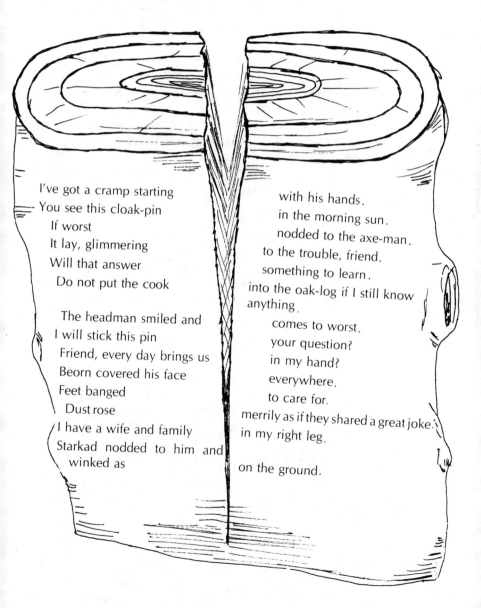

I've got a cramp starting
You see this cloak-pin
If worst
It lay, glimmering
Will that answer
Do not put the cook

The headman smiled and
I will stick this pin
Friend, every day brings us
Beorn covered his face
Feet banged
Dust rose
I have a wife and family
Starkad nodded to him and winked as

with his hands.
in the morning sun.
nodded to the axe-man.
to the trouble, friend.
something to learn.
into the oak-log if I still know anything.
comes to worst.
your question?
in my hand?
everywhere.
to care for.
merrily as if they shared a great joke.
in my right leg.
on the ground.

6. Guess the Gear

Here are items of gear and equipment from the passage:

longsword	knife	blade
helmet	arrows	cloak
belt	whetstone	cords
axe	pin	

Given one item, 'longsword', fit the rest of the items from the box into the spaces provided. Draw up 'longsword' and the criss-cross figure in your workbook.

7. Adjectives and Nouns in 'A Viking Raid'

Adjectives are words that describe nouns. However, in the following summary of *Horned Helmet* (from which the passage is taken) some of the most descriptive adjectives and some nouns have been removed. You'll notice they are gathered under the protection of the horned helmet itself.

Write the sentences with blanks in your workbook, putting in the missing adjectives as you go.

Horned Helmet

This is the story of Beorn, an .... boy who runs away from a .... master, is befriended by Starkad the .... Jomsviking, and joins his ....

As the Vikings make their .... raids along the Scottish .... Beorn learns to fight, and kill, to sing their songs, and to accept their .... code. Jomsvikings are not concerned with manners, only with truth and hard-dealing. Never talk to a Jomsviking just for the sake of ....

'We have sworn an oath only to say what is so; no more and no less.'

There is no .... in this book. It is a magnificent .... of the Norsemen, showing both their courage and .... with a ring of truth.

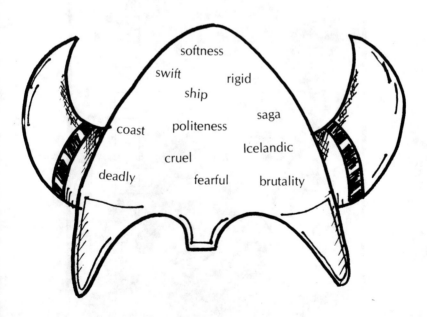

DINGO
THE STORY OF AN OUTLAW
Henry G Lamond

'One of the finest writers on wild life'
Times Literary Supplement

27. Death of a Roo

'Dingo' is the story of the struggle for survival of White Ears, a dingo hated and feared by man and beast. This passage vividly describes how White Ears and his mate kill a kangaroo.

When the 'roo had sped from them, White Ears and his mate dropped to an easy trot — the caste-mark of the dingo in action. They swung along, throwing distance behind them; with the inherent knowledge that time was on their side, that the crushing burden of fear was their ally, that distance meant nothing, they ran casually and seemingly without interest on the track the 'roo had taken. When they came up with him the second time they followed the same procedure: raced beside him so that he might be filled with the fear of death, then dropped back and ran casually after the buck had struck his gait and drawn away from them.

Three hours later, after a dozen flurried starts and frantic attempts to escape, the 'roo swung round for the last time and bailed up with his back against a tree as he looked in the direction from which he had come.

He was near his end. He knew it, and sought a place in which he could fight for his life. His eyes were wild and bloodshot; his chest and ribs flecked with strings of saliva; his arms dripping from repeated tongue dabbings; his flanks heaved. He was nerve-racked and exhausted; his energy drained by fear. His last spurt had been a short couple of hundred yards. He had just placed his back to a tree and drawn himself erect when the two dingoes stood before him.

The dogs were cool, collected, unperturbed; their mouths hardly panted. Almost, they ignored the 'roo. With an assumption of casual indifference, they picked out the most advantageous positions from which to attack.

The bitch lay ready a few yards away on the 'roo's left side, with her eyes steadily on him. White Ears took up a similar position on the opposite side. The bitch sprang to her feet, hurled herself at the waiting buck, caught herself in the air and sank to the ground just beyond his reach. She did it all in one action and like the crack of a whip.

The 'roo turned to meet that feint, swinging with a sweeping stroke of his gathering arms. Even as the buck commenced that action which he could not check, White Ears leapt in and took his prey under the armpit, from behind. As the stricken 'roo swayed, the bitch came in on the other side.

It was the end. The buck fought half-heartedly. He looked about him with dazed hopelessness; moved with the action of a marionette. Bereft of initiative defence, he fell in a tangled heap, the two dogs tearing at his throat while convulsive shudders ran through him.

The dingoes lapped the hot blood, which steamed in the cold air, and gulped lumps of quivering flesh.

HENRY G. LAMOND, *Dingo*

1. Reading for Meaning

(a) Can you explain why the dingoes seemed to have such a casual attitude to the pursuit of the 'roo?

(b) Why had the 'roo placed his back to a tree?

(c) Find evidence to show that the kangaroo was tired by the chase.

(d) Find evidence to suggest that the dogs had not been exhausted by the chase.

(e) What did you learn about the nature of the 'roo in this story?

(f) What did you learn about the natures of the dingoes?

(g) What plan of attack did the dingoes use to kill the 'roo?

(h) What is your reaction to dingoes after reading this story?

(i) Do you think the 'roo should have fought more courageously? Why?

(j) What is the meaning of (i) dazed (ii) frantic (iii) inherent (iv) ally? (Use the back-of-the-book dictionary to help you.)

2. Using Your Own Words

Write down these sentences, replacing the words in heavy (bold) type with words of your own that are similar in meaning.

(a) When they **came up with** him the second time, they **followed the same procedure.**
(b) He **sought** a place in which he could **struggle** for his life.
(c) He had just **drawn himself erect** when the two dingoes stood **before** him.
(d) The bitch **sprang** to her feet, **hurled** herself at the **waiting** buck, caught herself in the air and sank to the ground just **beyond** his reach.
(e) As the **stricken** 'roo **swayed,** the bitch came in on the other side.
(f) He was **near his end.**
(g) He was **nerve-racked** and **exhausted**; his energy **drained by fear.**
(h) His **last spurt** had been a short couple of hundred yards.

3. Match the Meanings

Match up the words in the first column with their meanings in the second column. Referring to the story itself will help you.

	WORDS FROM THE STORY	MEANINGS
(a)	caste-mark	a puppet on strings
(b)	gaped	calm
(c)	indifference	sides
(d)	unperturbed	particular feature
(e)	marionette	pretended attack
(f)	flanks	deprived
(g)	feint	agitated
(h)	flurried	absence of feeling
(i)	convulsive	opened
(j)	bereft	shaking violently

SPELLING WORDS		
casually	assumption	defence
procedure	advantageous	unperturbed
knowledge	similar	indifference
direction	commenced	quivering
exhausted	initiative	position

The next three exercises all depend on this box of spelling words.

4. Using the Correct Forms

Write down each of these sentences, inserting the correct form of the word in brackets.

(a) It was to the dingoes' .... to casually pursue the 'roo. [advantageous]

(b) .... finally forced the 'roo to stop trying to outdistance his pursuers. [exhausted]

(c) When the dingoes had the 'roo trapped, they .... to kill him. [procedure]

(d) The dingoes always .... they would catch the 'roo. [assumption]

(e) On several occasions the dingoes seemed .... to the 'roo. [indifference]

(f) The dingoes finally .... their attack on the buck. [initiative]

(g) The dingoes adopted a .... approach in the pursuit of the 'roo. [casually]

(h) The 'roo .... himself against a tree. [position]

5. Scrambled Spelling

Unscramble the following words from the spelling list opposite.

(a) r m a s l i i
(b) t v n i i i a e t
(c) c e e n d f
(d) g l o n k w e e d
(e) n i t o p s i o
(f) l a y s l u c a
(g) r o t i c e n i d
(h) u s i n o t p a s m

6. Suitable Words

Write down these sentences and, in the blank spaces, insert the most suitable words from the spelling list. Don't use any word more than once.

(a) Even though the 'roo was .... he sought a place which would be .... for him.
(b) The dingoes always seemed .... and waited some time before taking the ....
(c) The bitch .... the attack from the 'roo's left side.
(d) The dingoes could afford to .... pursue the 'roo because they had the .... that they would eventually catch their prey.
(e) The 'roo had no real .... against the .... of attack adopted by the dingoes.
(f) A person reading *Dingo* could readily make the .... that the dingoes had made a .... attack before.

7. Complete the Table

Copy down the table and fill in the blank spaces.

	NOUN	VERB	ADJECTIVE	ADVERB
(a)			convulsive	
(b)			repeated	
(c)	energy	energise		
(d)	initiative		initial	
(e)	action			
(f)	direction			
(g)				steadily
(h)	defence			

8. Homophones

The following pairs of words have the same sounds but different meanings. See whether you can insert them correctly in the sentences.

| check | gait | feint | prey |
| cheque | gate | faint | pray |

(a) The 'roo was the dingoes' ....
(b) The .... of the dingoes was casual.
(c) The dingoes did not need to .... whether the 'roo was going fast or slowly.
(d) A dingo-trapper could earn a large .... for killing dingoes.
(e) At times the reader could be tempted to .... for the kangaroo.
(f) The kangaroo seemed about to .... after the arduous pursuit.
(g) The .... of the bitch led to the quick death of the 'roo.
(h) There was no farm .... through which the 'roo could escape.

Dictionary

- The part of speech of each dictionary word is given.
- Parts of speech are abbreviated as follows:

n	noun	pr p	present participle
n pl	noun plural	pp	past participle
adj	adjective	adv	adverb
v	verb		

- Where a word has several possible meanings which are given, these are numbered.
- Other forms of the word have been bracketed.

accoutrements n pl equipment, gear
activated pp made active [activate v; activation n]
admirable adj excellent, worthy of being reported [admire v; admiration n]
admit v (1) to own up, (2) to allow entrance [admittance n]
advise v to offer counsel [advice n (opinion or information given); advisory adj]
aggressive adj disposed (tending) to attack [aggression n; aggressively adv]
aimlessly adv without aim or purpose [aimless adj]
alacrity n quickness, readiness
allegiance n personal loyalty or trust given to a leader
ally n (or v) helper, aid, friend [alliance n]
alternative n a choice between two or more things [alternatively adv]
altimeter n aeronautical instrument for measuring height above sea level
amiably adv in a friendly way [amiable adj]
analysed pp taken apart and examined [analyse v; analytically adv; analysis n; analytical adj]
anew adj again, in a different way
anonymous adj without any name [anonymity n]
anticipation n expectation, capacity to foresee or prepare for beforehand [anticipate v; anticipated pp]
appalling pr p terrifying, causing dismay [appal v; appalled pp]
apparition n a weird appearance — such as that of a ghost
arrayed pp set out, laid out — as for a display [array v (n)]
astride adv sitting or standing with the legs on either side of something
autism n the condition of being wrapped up in one's own world and out of touch with the outside world [autistic adj]
automatic adj working by machinery alone [automation n; automatically adv]
awkward adj clumsy [awkwardly adv; awkwardness n]

banished pp exiled, sent away [banish v; banishment n]
bank v (1) to dip one wing — as for turning, (2) to deposit money [bank n; banking pr p]
bared pp revealed, shown, exposed [bare v; bareness n]
basking pr p enjoying warmth and light [bask v]
bayonet n a short sword usually fixed to a rifle
bear n a large furry animal; v to carry
berserk adj wild, in a mad frenzy — as in 'go berserk'
bespattered pp hit by droplets, partly smeared [bespatter v]
billowed pp rose, swelled, rolled — as with smoke, dust, spray [billow v (n); billowing pr p]
blanch v to turn white, to go pale [blanched pp]
blood-curdling adj terrifying, horrible — so horrific as to seem to curdle or congeal the blood
borne pp carried [bear v]
brace v to strengthen [brace n; bracing pr p]
breakneck adj dangerous — as in 'breakneck speed'
brewery n a place where beer is made (brewed) [brew v]
brine n salt water
brutality n savageness, cruelty [brutalise v; brute n; brutal adj]
burglar n a person who breaks into a house or other premises to steal [burgle v; burglary n]

callous adj cruel, unfeeling [callousness n]
carcass n dead body
careen v (1) to turn a ship on its side in order to scrape its hull, (2) to career wildly (of vehicle)
cautiously adv carefully, with attention to safety [caution n; cautious adj]
chalet n a wooden cottage
changeable adj likely to alter, irregular [change v (n)]
charred pp blackened with fire on the outside [char v]
chum v to drop live bait into the sea to attract fish
circled pp went round and round [circle v (n); circular adj]
clenched pp grasped firmly [clench v]
colander n a perforated (pierced with holes) dish or bowl used as a strainer in cooking
competent adj properly qualified, able [competence n; competently adv]
composed pp (1) arranged in a calm and controlled way, (2) created (as in music) [compose v; composition n]
concentrating pr p (1) thinking hard, (2) bringing together at one point [concentrate v; concentration n]
confusion n disorder [confused pp; confuse v; confusing pr p]
constantly adv unchangingly, the same all the time [constant adj (n)]
conveyed pp carried [convey v; conveyance n]
crises n pl moments of extreme danger, difficulty, trouble [crisis n; critical adj; critically adv]

dazed pp stunned, stupefied, benumbed [daze n]
decision n a definite conclusion [decisively adv; decide v; decisive adj]
demurely adv coyly and meekly [demure adj]
detached pp apart — one thing taken away from another [detach v; detachable adj; detachment n]
device n (1) a plan, a scheme, (2) a contrivance, or contraption
devise v to plan, contrive
devour v to consume or eat up
de-weapon v to take the weapon away
discharge n an unloading, a release [discharge v]
disclose v to reveal [disclosure n]
disintegrate v to break up into parts [disintegration n]
distinctly adv plainly, clearly [distinct adj]
distract v to draw away, or divert (the interest or attention) [distraction n; distracting pr p]
distraught pp violently agitated
dutiful adj willing in obedience and service [duty n]

ebbed pp flowed away, receded [ebb v; ebbing pr p]
embers n pl small pieces of live coal or glowing wood from a fire
engorged pp crammed full, over-filled [engorge v]
engulf v to swallow up [engulfed pp]
entertainment n (1) amusement, (2) show or performance [entertain v; entertainer n; entertainingly adv]
entire adj whole, complete, all [entirety n; entirely adv]
epidiascope n an optical lantern which projects images of opaque and transparent objects
eruption n a bursting forth, a breaking out [erupt v]
eventually adv finally, at length, at last [eventual adj]
exertion n effort [exert v]
expanding pr p getting larger, swelling [expand v; expansive adj; expansion n; expansively adv]
expired pp (1) breathed out, (2) died, (3) elapsed [expiry n]
extensions n pl additional parts [extend v; extensive adj; extensively adv]
extraordinarily adv uncommonly, unusually [extraordinary adj]

few n (adj) not very many
flailing pr p whipping, thrashing, whipping around [flail n (v)]
flaps n pl the broad, hinged pieces of metal on a plane's wings used to make it rise or fall
formidable adj to be feared
fragment n a small part of something [fragment v]
frantic adj wildly excited, frenzied [frantically adv]
froth n (v) foam, small bubbles

gallop n (or v) the fastest speed of a horse
gesticulating pr p making wild movements with the hand(s), waving the hands around [gesticulation n; gesticulate v]
gig n (1) a light, one-horse carriage with two wheels, (2) a ship's boat
gosling n a baby goose
grime n dirt ingrained in some surface [grimy adj]
gruesome adj causing one to shudder, horrible, frightful [gruesomeness n]
gyroscope n an instrument used to employ or demonstrate rotation or spin [gyroscopic adj]

halo n a circle or crown of light round the head of an angel or saint
harshness n roughness, severity [harsh adj; harshly adv]
hauled pp pulled, dragged [haul v; haulage n]
havoc n destruction, devastation
hearth n the floor of a fireplace
heroically adv like a hero [heroic adj]
hesitate v to be undecided, to pause uncertainly [hesitation n]
hilariously adv uproariously, mirthfully [hilarity n; hilarious adj]
horoscope n an observation of the sky and planets at a certain time — used to fortell the future by astrologers
host n (1) a large number, (2) one who entertains another
hostile adj unfriendly, opposed
hostility n opposition, animosity

ignore v to take no notice of [ignorance n; ignorant adj; ignorantly adv]
illiterate adj unable to read or write [illiteracy n]
inarticulate adj unable to speak distinctly or well [inarticulateness n]
indifference n absence of interest or attention [indifferent adj; indifferently adv]
indignantly adv angrily, in a very displeased manner [indignant adj; indignation n]
inevitability n the impossibility of avoiding; the certainty (of a happening) [inevitable adj; inevitably adv]
inherent adj fixed in, situated in, anything that is an essential part of something else [inherently adv]
injured pp hurt, wounded [injury n; injurious adj; injure v]
inlet n a small arm or extension of a sea or river
instant n a moment in time [instant adj; instantly adv]
instinctively adv using natural impulse or inborn knowledge, not based on experience [instinct n; instinctive adj]
intensity n high degree of energy; force, ardency [intense adj; intensely adv]
intimately adv personally, closely [intimacy n; intimate adj]
intrigued pp interested — in the sense that one's curiosity is aroused

lank adj long, thin and lean
laryngoscope n a mirror, apparatus or tool for examining a person's larynx (part of the throat)
license v to allow or grant permit [licence n]
limp adj (1) without stiffness, without life, (2) v to drag one foot when walking [limpness n; limply adv]
literal adj following the exact words [literally adv]
lob v to send or throw with a high-pitched motion
loping pr p running with long, bounding strides
loyalty n faithfulness, allegiance [loyal adj; loyally adv]
ludicrously adv ridiculously, comically, laughably [ludicrous adj]
lurched pp leaned suddenly to one side, staggered [lurch v]

macaroni n Italian food made of flour, egg and water — e.g. spaghetti
magneto n an electrical generator that uses magnets to produce a current
maintenance n (1) support; regular care, (2) money paid to support someone [maintain v]
malevolence n evil, malice [malevolent adj]
massive adj large and heavy
matted pp tangled and knotted — as with hair
medical adj maintaining health, curing disease [medicine n; medically adv; medicate v]
might n power, strength [mighty adj; mightily adv]
mischievous adj inclined to act in playful but annoying ways [mischief n]
missile n an object fired or thrown
momentarily adv for a brief period of time, taking only a moment [moment n]
momentum n the impetus (force) gained by something moving
monotonous adj essentially the same, boring [monotony n; monotonously adv]
monstrous adj like a monster, huge, unnatural [monster n; monstrosity n]
motion n movement

nimbus n a cloud or mist
nothing n not a single thing
now adv at the present time

obelisk n a tapering shape, usually in stone — often used as a memorial stone
occupy v to live in, to take position in [occupation n]
offshore adj on the seaward side of the shore

pacifically adv in a peaceful way, trying to make (or keep) peace [pacifism n; pacific adj; pacify v]
participants n pl those who take part — especially in a game or sport [participant n; participation n; participate v]
pause n a short rest or stop before continuing [pause v]

pavement n footpath, sidewalk
paws n pl the feet of an animal
peculiar adj strange [peculiarity n]
peered pp looked narrowly or intently [peer v]
penetrate v to find an entry or access, to pierce [penetration n]
phenomenon n a remarkable or rare thing or happening [phenomenal adj; phenomenally adv; phenomena n pl]
pierce v to penetrate
plead v to make an earnest appeal [plea n]
plummeted pp plunged [plummet v]
plunged pp dived, fell [plunge v]
pores n pl tiny holes in the skin through which sweat passes
poult n a baby turkey
pours v tips or flows out — as with liquid
practise v to perform habitually in order to gain skill [practised pp; practice n]
prairie n a great, treeless expanse of grasslands
predicament n a dangerous or uncomfortable situation
primeval adj primitive, belonging to the first ages of time
proffered pp offered, usually as a gift [proffer v]
profile n a side view of the face
protective adj intended to defend or prevent from harm [protect v; protectively adv; protection n]
prow n the front part of a boat
prying pr p (1) forcing open by leverage, (2) seeking to interfere in another person's affairs [pry v]

quiet adj with little noise or sound [quiet n; quietness n; quieten v; quietly adv]
quite adv completely, entirely

rampaging pr p behaving violently and destructively [rampage v]
rawhide n untanned leather
rebellious adj defying authority [rebellion n; rebel n; rebel v]
recognition n (1) fame that is deserved, (2) seeing someone or something that is familiar [recognise v]
remorse n sorrow for a wrong that has been done [remorseful adj]
rending pr p tearing, ripping [rend v]
reposed pp rested [repose v or n]
repulsed pp driven back, made to retreat [repulse v]
resentful adj showing hurt feelings [resentment n; resent v; resentfully adv]
retrieved pp regained possession of
rippler n a fishing term used to describe the rippling water that marks or shows a school of fish
route n the way taken to get to some place

sarcastic adj making bitter, ironic remarks [sarcasm n; sarcastically adv]
searing pr p scorching, burning [sear v]
security n safety from danger [secure adj; secure v; securely adv]
separate adj (v) unconnected, distinct, divided from the rest [separation n; separately adv]
sequence n a connected series of happenings or events
sextant n an instrument used in navigation to measure angular distances
shrivel v to wither into a wrinkled state
shrugged pp raised the shoulders — as when expressing lack of interest or hopelessness [shrug v or n]
sibilant adj hissing [n a hissing sound]
siege n the period when an army surrounds a city or fortress to force it to surrender
sieve n an object used to separate finer from coarser particles [sieve v]
singe v to burn slightly [singed pp; singeing pr p]
sluggish adj slow-moving, tired, sluglike [sluggishly adv]
smarted pp stung, pained [smart v]
smouldering pr p burning without flames [smoulder v]
snarled pp made an angry sound, spoken harshly [snarl v (n); snarling pr p]
solder n a kind of soft metal which is melted and used to join other metals
sole adj the one and only
solution n (1) answer to a problem, (2) a liquid in which a chemical is dissolved [solve v; soluble adj; solubility n]
soon adv in the near future
sophistication n the quality of being worldly wise, not simple [sophisticated pp]
sought pp searched for, looked for [seek v]
soul n the spiritual part of a person
spaghetti n a kind of macaroni
spectroscope n an instrument for examining the spectra (colours) of light rays
stance n any particular way of standing
stereoscope n an instrument for viewing a pair of photos of the same object taken from slightly different angles to give a 3D effect
stethoscope n an instrument used for listening to a person's heart
stifle (1) n the knee joint of a horse, (2) v to choke or suffocate
storey n one of the floors of a house or block
strewn pp scattered around
stubborn adj obstinate, unyielding [stubbornness n; stubbornly adv]
subdue v to conquer, overcome, quieten [subdued pp]
successor n the one who follows or comes next in line
suffusion n colour appearing from within as with a blush or flush of rage on the face [suffuse v]

tactics n pl plan of attack or procedure aimed at achieving something
talons n pl claws (of a bird)

tantrum n a display of temper
taut adj tight, not slack [tautness n; tauten v]
thong n (1) a strip of leather (e.g. used as a belt), (2) one of a pair of thongs or rubber footwear
threaten v to menace
threshold n edge, entrance
tilt v (n) incline, slope, slant [tilting pr p; tilted pp]
tottered pp wobbled, walked unsteadily [totter v]
tried pp made an effort, attempted [try n (v); trying pr p]

ultimate adj final [ultimately adv]
unattractive adj not pleasant to look at
unerringly adv without making any errors, steadily
unexpectedly adv without any warning
ungainly adj clumsy
unruffled adj calm, composed
unseen adj hidden from sight
urgency n great need [urgently adv; urgent adj]
utterly adv completely [utter adj]

veer v to change direction
vehemently adv with strong feeling, forcefully, violently [vehement adj]
vicinity n the surrounding area
viciousness n evil, nastiness, brutality [vicious adj; viciously adv]
vitamin n a component of many foods — essential to health
vortex n a spinning tunnel

winced pp moved — as in pain; flinched [wince v (n)]
wrath n anger [wrathful adj]
wrenching pr p twisting or pulling to one side violently [wrench v (n)]

zoology n the scientific study of animals [zoological adj]

Acknowledgements

The authors and publishers are grateful to the following for permission to reproduce extracts from copyright material.

Methuen Children's Books Ltd and Associated Book Publishers Ltd for *Little House on the Prairie* by Laura Ingalls Wilder; Angus & Robertson Publishers for *To the Wild Sky* by Ivan Southall, and for 'How Would I Be' from *The Yarns of Billy Borker* by Frank Hardy; Macdonald and Jane's Publishers Ltd for *Midnite* by Randolph Stow; Hamish Hamilton Ltd for *Charlotte's Web* by E. B. White, and for *Freaky Friday* by Mary Rodgers; Rigby Limited for *Blue Fin* by Colin Thiele; Penguin Books Ltd for *Island of the Blue Dolphins* by Scott O'Dell © 1960 (Longman Young Books, 1961, Puffin Books, 1960); Hutchinson Publishing Group Limited for *The Nargun and The Stars* by Patricia Wrightson; The Bodley Head for *The Cay* by Theodore Taylor, for *Dragon Slayer* by Rosemary Sutcliffe, and for *My Side of the Mountain* by Jean George; Hodder & Stoughton (Australia) Pty Limited for *Wildfire* by Mavis Thorpe Clark; George G. Harrap & Company Ltd for *The Goal-Keeper's Revenge* by Bill Naughton; Jonathan Cape Ltd for *The Silver Sword* by Ian Serraillier; Bolt & Watson Ltd for *The Brumby* by M. E. Patchett; Hodder & Stoughton Children's Books for *Children on the Oregon Trail* by A. Rutgers van der Loeff, and *The Horned Helmet* by Henry Treece; Macmillan Publishers Ltd, London and Basingstoke, for *The Dolphin Crossing* by Jill Paton Walsh, and for *Sam and Me* by Joan Tate; William Heinemann Ltd for *Dorp Dead* by Julia Cunningham; Collins Publishers for *Beasts in my Belfry* by Gerald Durrell; Faber & Faber Limited for *The Men from P.I.G. and R.O.B.O.T.* by Harry Harrison; Hope, Leresche & Sayle for *Dingo*, copyright © 1945 by Henry G. Lamond; Oxford University Press for *A Dog Called George* by Margaret Balderson, for *The October Child* by Eleanor Spence, and for *Flambards* by K. M. Peyton.

Penguin Books Ltd, *vi*, 6, 22, 30, 48, 56, 70, 80, 88, 102, 110, 124, 130, 138, 146, 156, 184, 192; Oxford University Press, pp. 14, 62; Rigby Limited, p. 40; Hodder & Stoughton Children's Books, p. 94; Angus & Robertson Publishers, p. 116; Joan Tate and Macmillan Publishers Ltd, p. 160; William Heinemann Ltd, p. 168; Fontana Paperbacks, p. 174; Sun Books Pty Ltd, p. 202.

While every care has been taken to trace and acknowledge copyright, the publishers tender their apologies for any accidental infringement where copyright has proved untraceable. They would be pleased to come to a suitable arrangement with the rightful owner in each case.